GUIDELINES

T 3

017

Commissioned by **David Spriggs**

The Bible Reading Fellowship
15 The Chambers, Vineyard
Abingdon OX14 3FE
brf.org.uk

The Bible Reading Fellowship (BRF) is a Registered Charity (233280)

ISBN 978 0 85746 450 7

Distributed in Australia by:
MediaCom Education Inc, PO Box 610, Unley, SA 5061
Tel: 1 800 811 311 | admin@mediacom.org.au

Distributed in New Zealand by:
Scripture Union Wholesale, PO Box 760, Wellington
Tel: 04 385 0421 | suwholesale@clear.net.nz

Acknowledgements

Printed by Gutenberg Press, Tarxien, Malta

Suggestions for using *Guidelines*

Set aside a regular time and place, if possible, when you can read and pray undisturbed. Before you begin, take time to be still and, if you find it helpful, use the BRF Prayer on page 6.

In *Guidelines*, the introductory section provides context for the passages or themes to be studied, while the units of comment can be used daily, weekly, or whatever best fits your timetable. You will need a Bible (more than one if you want to compare different translations) as Bible passages are not included. At the end of each week is a 'Guidelines' section, offering further thoughts about, or practical application of what you have been studying.

Occasionally, you may read something in *Guidelines* that you find particularly challenging, even uncomfortable. This is inevitable in a series of notes which draws on a wide spectrum of contributors, and doesn't believe in ducking difficult issues. Indeed, we believe that *Guidelines* readers much prefer thought-provoking material to a bland diet that only confirms what they already think.

If you do disagree with a contributor, you may find it helpful to go through these three steps. First, think about why you feel uncomfortable. Perhaps this is an idea that is new to you, or you are not happy at the way something has been expressed. Or there may be something more substantial—you may feel that the writer is guilty of sweeping generalisation, factual error, theological or ethical misjudgment. Second, pray that God would use this disagreement to teach you more about his word and about yourself. Third, think about what you will do as a result of the disagreement. You might resolve to find out more about the issue, or write to the contributor or the editors of *Guidelines*.

To send feedback, you may email or write to BRF at the addresses shown opposite. If you would like your comment to be included on our website, please email connect@brf.org.uk. You can also Tweet to @brfonline, using the hashtag #brfconnect.

Writers in this issue

Nigel G. Wright was Principal of Spurgeon's College from 2000 to 2013 and is a former President of the Baptist Union of Great Britain. He has written *Jesus Christ—the Alpha and the Omega* for BRF (2010).

Mark Scarlata is Tutor and Lecturer in Old Testament Studies at St Mellitus College. Mark grew up in the USA and did his theological studies at Gordon-Conwell Theological Seminary and Yale Divinity School.

Alec Gilmore, a Baptist minister and a frequent contributor to *Guidelines*. has contributed to many Christian publications in the UK and US. His most recent book is *A Concise Dictionary of Bible Origins and Interpretation* (T&T Clark/Continuum).

Alistair Wilson teaches New Testament and Greek at the Highland Theological College in Scotland. Alistair holds a PhD in New Testament studies from the University of Aberdeen and is a minister of the Free Church of Scotland.

Martyn Percy is Dean of Christ Church, Oxford. He is also a member of the Faculty of Theology at Oxford University and Professor of Theological Education at King's College London. He writes and teaches on modern ecclesiology.

Michael Parsons is a commissioning editor for The Bible Reading Fellowship. He is the author of several books on the Reformation and an Associate Research Fellow at Spurgeon's College, London. He has written *Praying the Bible with Luther* for BRF.

Matthew van Duyvenbode is Director of National Programme & Research at Bible Society. A graduate in Theology, he directs Bible Society's engagement in public life, including the arts, education, media and politics.

Sarah Beresford is joint Director of the Catholic Bible School in West Sussex. She is studying for a Masters Degree in Christian Ministry at the University of Chichester.

Jeremy Duff is Principal of St Padarn's Institute, a new centre for ministry training in Wales. His book *The Elements of New Testament Greek* (2005) is Cambridge University Press's bestselling religion title. He has also written *Peter's Preaching* for BRF (2015).

David Spriggs has retired from Bible Society but continues his work with them as a consultant. His main role is as a team minister at the Hinckley Baptist Church, with special responsibility to work with the leaders.

David Spriggs writes...

Halfway through this four-month period comes 31 October, All Saints' Day, and this year it is especially significant. Five hundred years ago, a young man named Martin Luther marched up to the Castle Church at Wittenberg and nailed to the door his '95 Theses'—a normal way to start a theological discussion. Many scholars see this as the start of the Protestant Reformation proper, which has shaped our country and our own lives and desire to read the Bible for ourselves.

At the heart of Luther's new understanding of the Christian faith was his reading of scripture. In order to commemorate this event and all that flows from it we have commissioned three special sets of notes. The radical understanding that God 'justifies' sinners by his grace and through their faith in Christ alone was a liberating new truth for Luther. Alistair Wilson, who teaches theology in Scotland, engages with some key scriptural passages as well as some contemporary debate about their significance.

Luther was not all theology and controversy! He had a deep spirituality, and the other two contributions help us benefit from it. First, Professor Martyn Percy, Dean of Christ Church Oxford, introduces us to some of Luther's favourite psalms and allows us to experience the riches of his devotional heart. Then, Mike Parsons, Commissioning Editor at BRF, helps us to appreciate Luther's understanding of and practice of prayer. Mike has taught systematic theology in Australia; you can find out more about Mike and the way that scripture has shaped his own life in the 'Author profile'.

We value the Old Testament as part of our scriptural 'feeding'. In this issue we have our respected friend Alec Gilmore relating Numbers to our situations. Also, a new writer for us, Mark Scarlata, explores insights for leaders from the life of Moses. If this were not enough for one issue, we begin with Nigel Wright, who completes his contributions on Matthew's Gospel, ending, of course, with the commission of Jesus for us to take the good new to all nations. Matthew van Duyvenbode writes for us on Thessalonians, providing a fascinating insight to how the task of mission was carried out by Paul and his friends. Of course, we have not neglected the Advent season. Sarah Beresford focuses on 'God's Advent call', Jeremy Duff unpacks the incarnation in John's Gospel, while I explore some of the rich Christian words within the Christmas story in Luke 2:8–20.

This issue marks a very special anniversary but it is also full of great biblical riches. Please encourage your friends to get hold of a copy as well as reading it with profit yourselves.

The BRF Prayer

Almighty God,
you have taught us that your word is a lamp for our feet
and a light for our path. Help us, and all who prayerfully
read your word, to deepen our fellowship with you
and with each other through your love.
And in so doing may we come to know you more fully,
love you more truly, and follow more faithfully
in the steps of your son Jesus Christ, who lives and reigns
with you and the Holy Spirit, one God for evermore.
Amen

A Prayer for Remembrance

We commit ourselves to work in penitence and faith for reconciliation
between the nations, that all people may, together, live in freedom,
justice and peace. We pray for all who in bereavement, disability and
pain continue to suffer the consequences of fighting and terror. We
remember with thanksgiving and sorrow those whose lives, in world
wars and conflicts past and present, have been given and taken away.

From An Order of Service for Remembrance Sunday,
Churches Together in Britain and Ireland 2005

Matthew 24—28

Each of the Gospels has been described, with some warrant, as 'a Passion narrative with an introduction'. Attention is drawn in this way to the amount of space devoted in each Gospel to the last week of Jesus' life. Matthew is no exception. Jesus has already entered Jerusalem in chapter 21, so roughly a quarter of the action is placed in the last week of his life. Within this framework we find an extensive array of parables, teaching, debates and activities before the climactic events of arrest, trial, crucifixion and resurrection.

Every aspect of Jesus' life is significant for us if we believe, as Christians do, that in him God is personally present among us. But this focus on the last week indicates that, theologically, there is much to occupy us here. Jesus is prophet, teacher, wonder-worker, healer and Messiah, but he is also much more. In giving himself up to death on the cross, he is acting to make atonement for the sins of the world. There is something necessary about the journey he makes to Jerusalem. It has to be this way. He will not allow himself to be deflected from this calling and requirement. It goes against every human expectation: he deliberately puts himself in harm's way. We do not expect the Messiah to come to such an end. He is supposed to triumph, to succeed, to vanquish, yet his life ends in a miserable, criminal's death, in dejection and rejection. Yet beyond this is the inscrutable will of the all-wise God, the Father of Jesus Christ, who is working out a saving purpose even through the self-emptying and vulnerability of the Son.

If this remarkable story had not been given to us as it is, we could never have invented it. No doubt this is why it has captured the imagination of so many people of so many different kinds—not of Christians alone—throughout the 2000 years it has been in circulation. However many times we revisit it, it still has something to say to us. It is a mystery—not that it makes no sense, but that it can never be exhausted. It is profound and unfathomable and so requires us to read it with humility.

Quotations are from the New Revised Standard Version.

1 Preparing for judgement

Matthew 24:1–14

Chapters 24 and 25 are largely concerned with the judgement that is to fall upon Jerusalem as a prelude to the final judgement that will bring the world to its ultimate goal. Chapters such as these, which belong generally to the literary category called 'apocalyptic', can be hard for us to appreciate because of their dramatic and somewhat frightening nature. Catastrophe, which literally means the 'overturning' of the established order, is part of their character. They also tend to telescope the future so that, from the vantage point of the speaker, near events are seen against the backdrop of the final judgement of which they are a sign. In this case, Jesus speaks of the destruction of the temple in AD70 but sees beyond it to his own final coming and 'the end of the age' (v. 3).

Herod's temple, fully visible from the Mount of Olives (v. 3), which was itself closely associated with fulfilled prophecy (Zechariah 14:4), was still being built. Yet Jesus foresaw its total dismantling by the Romans (v. 2). Today only a retaining wall, known as the Wailing or Western Wall, which shored up the mountain on which the temple stood, remains visible. Jesus was proven tragically correct.

This premonition is the trigger for further sober warnings about the future that awaits the disciples. There will be wars, earthquakes and famines. False messiahs and prophets will arise and the disciples themselves will be cruelly persecuted. Some who have believed in Jesus will lose their love and fall away (v. 12). This is not a happy picture.

When such things happen today, people sometimes say, 'The end of the world must be near', yet Jesus explicitly denies this in verse 6. Rather, such events are the stock in trade of a troubled world and are to be expected. Within this scenario there are two priorities. The first is to endure to the end (v. 13), to hold fast to the faith and stay true to Christ, come what may. The second is to proclaim the good news of Christ to all nations across the world. The end will not come until this work has been done (v. 14). Jesus' encouragement to us, then, rather than indulging in fruitless speculation about times and seasons (Acts 1:7), is to get on with the job that he began.

2 History repeats itself

Matthew 24:15–28

One of the most traumatic of many traumatic events in the history of Israel took place in 168 or 167BC, when Antiochus Epiphanes set up an altar to Zeus in the Jewish temple and offered pig's blood upon it. This is what is meant by the 'desolating sacrilege' in verse 15 (see Daniel 9:27; 11:31). Jesus warned that this or a similar act would be repeated, and the fact that 'when' in verse 15 has the force of 'whenever' suggests that several events may have been in view. Suggested candidates have been the bringing of Roman standards into the temple with their images of Caesar; the attempt by Caligula to erect his own image in the temple in AD40 (prevented only by his assassination); and the desecration of the temple with human blood in the Jewish revolt of AD66–70. Whatever is intended (and Jesus' hearers knew better than we), when these things happened it would be time to flee the city without delay (vv. 16–21).

The strange saying about vultures in verse 28 may give the clue to what is happening here. The word used for 'vultures' is literally 'eagles', and so it probably refers to the eagle standards of the Roman legions descending like vultures on the corpse of Jerusalem. Having been infuriated by the Jewish rebels, they were in no mood to seek peace. This was not a time to hang around. In fact, we know that Christians forsook the city in those days. They had been forewarned.

In times of crisis, religion also becomes more extreme and deranged, so Jesus warned his disciples against the claims they would hear from false messiahs and prophets (v. 24). They could be assured that when the Son of Man came, his coming, like the lightning, would be unmistakable and clear (v. 27). It would not be a secret thing, known to only a few. Although given for a time of crisis, this guidance applies to all places and times.

Tragic though the destruction of the temple was, it was also a vindication of what Jesus had said. His warnings came to pass, and the event was brutal in its ferocity. No wonder Jesus wept over Jerusalem. Had his generation heeded his message of refusing to counter evil with evil, things might have turned out very differently.

3 Timing the end

Now Jesus lifts his eyes beyond the destruction of Jerusalem to a greater crisis, of which the fall of the temple will be only a foretaste. The sign of the Son of Man will appear (v. 30). This is an example of how apocalyptic ways of speaking can telescope events, seeing near occurrences in the light of those that are further away. The fact that Jesus says, 'Immediately after…' (v. 29) has led some to think, not unreasonably, that Jesus saw his own coming as the Son of Man following hard on Jerusalem's fall. In that case, Jesus would be mistaken. Yet what are we to make of his saying that only the Father knows the time of his coming (v. 36), or the suggestion that people will be living routine and ordered lives before they are taken by surprise by his coming (vv. 37–42), or that his coming may actually be delayed (v. 48)?

There are mysteries here and they are best resolved, if resolve them we can, by better understanding the nature of apocalyptic writing. Ascribing chronological proximity is a way of speaking of the urgency and importance of the spiritual realities that press in upon us. Christ's coming is described as 'near, at the very gates' (v. 33) because we should not put off thinking about or preparing for it. We must live in the light of it, and do so this very moment. The stars are about to 'fall from heaven' (v. 29), meaning not that the physical universe will suddenly fall apart but that we are dealing with earth-shaking events that will change the course of history, whose significance we cannot afford to ignore.

There is a further challenge to our understanding in the claim that 'this generation' will not pass away before the events described have taken place (v. 34). Certainly the generation Jesus was addressing, shortly before AD30, would largely live on to endure the distress of the fall of Jerusalem. But what about his greater coming as lightning across the sky? By 'this generation', Jesus could mean the Jewish nation, which survives still, despite all the events of the fall of Jerusalem and much more. Or is it his way of saying that the human race will live to see these things? Perhaps his understanding was more open-ended than we imagine.

4 Staying alert

Although these verses contain a number of uncertainties, there is actually a very clear and practical message here. We should stay alert and be ready to meet the Lord when he comes (24:46). When he does come, it will be at an unexpected time, and so we should expect the unexpected (v. 44). This is all the more imperative since, despite the suggestion that the Lord will come soon, there is an even greater indication that his coming will be delayed: his absence will go on longer than we think it should. This comes across both in the parable of the wicked servant who turns away to ungodly and unkind patterns of life because the master is delayed (vv. 48–49) and in the parable of the foolish bridesmaids who run out of oil for their lamps when the bridegroom fails to turn up on time (25:5). The fate of both is unfortunate (24:51; 25:10). We might feel it is unfair of the master and the bridegroom not to keep to time, but it is the privilege of both so to do. Both parables call into question the notion that Jesus expected to return within a very short time. From the beginning he planted the idea of his delay.

Being ready to meet the Lord does not mean being distracted from our other, legitimate, God-given tasks. The faithful and wise servant in 24:45 prepares for the master's coming by doing what is assigned to him, looking after the other servants. His commendation is based on the fact that he is busily working rather than gazing anxiously into the far-off distance (v. 46). By contrast, the wicked servant is spending his time selfishly and wastefully (v. 49). The bridesmaids are failing to fulfil their customary function by being inadequately prepared for the time delay.

The Christian life turns out, for all of us, to be a marathon rather than a sprint, and it calls for the capacity to 'endure to the end' (24:13). This must involve persevering through periods of opposition and conflict, avoiding wrong turnings and distractions along the way. The oil of enthusiasm for Christ and his teachings may have to stretch a long way. The challenge is to keep burning and to stay on the boil until the very end.

5 Good stewardship

Yet again Jesus tells a parable in which the negative outcome for the 'worthless slave' is quite extreme (v. 30), as in 24:51. As with so much of the Bible, we have to imagine this story being narrated and making its compelling impact upon its hearers. In verse 29 there is an astute depiction of the positive and negative aspects of capitalism, although this is unlikely to be the lesson behind the story. We are still in the realm of present and final judgement, and in both dimensions the concern is about what we have done with what we have been given. This was true for the nation of Israel facing judgement and it is true for all humanity, not least the church.

We have all been given something to work with, but not in equal amounts. The word 'talent' that occurs here in the NRSV has passed into the English language to mean more than a unit of currency. It has to do with the skills, endowments and opportunities that are bestowed upon us. All have been given something to work with in life. Although all people 'are created equal', they are also created unequal, since some have five talents, some two, and some only one. That's life. The important thing is what we do with what we have. A good and trustworthy servant puts his or her talents to work in order to make a return on them, and they are then returned to the one who gave them in the first place. The words 'enter into the joy of your master' (vv. 21, 23) have the resonance of heavenly as well as earthly reward. The 'wicked and lazy slave', by contrast (v. 26), is guilty not of misuse, but of sloth. It is not that he does something wrong but that he does nothing.

We are used to thinking of sin as rebellion or transgression, shaking the fist at God, but these actions require energy and a degree of defiance. This servant's sin was that he was afraid (v. 25) and hid his talent away. This too is sin, which may involve, in the words of the General Confession, 'the things we have done and the things we have left undone'. Apathy is an outrage to God and as much a rejection of our vocation as anything else.

6 Without thought of reward

Today's passage imagines the final judgement with the nations gathered before the glorious Son of Man. Palestinian sheep and goats resemble each other, but they can be distinguished by the fact that the tails of goats point upwards. The crucial decision concerns who will enter into the Father's kingdom and inherit eternal life, and who will go into eternal punishment (vv. 34, 41, 46). This is a serious business. It is true that life is full of shades of grey, but in the ultimate judgement there will be clarity: light and darkness; life and death; for and against. And how will our true nature be known? Through the conscious and unconscious deeds that we have done.

Is Jesus teaching salvation by works? It almost reads that way, but it is more about *judgement* by works. We are judged by what we do rather than what we claim. 'Lord, Lord' is not enough (7:21; 25:11). It is more likely the case, therefore, that the works of love described here are evidence of the trustful orientation towards God that we call faith. Faith works itself out in love (1 Timothy 1:5). The striking feature of the righteous is that their works of love are spontaneous and done for their own sake rather than for the expectation of a reward. Yet rewarded they are, as they open up the way to life. By contrast, the unrighteous are unaware of the needs that are staring them in the face (v. 44).

How is it, then, that Jesus speaks of the works of love having been done to his very self (vv. 35–36, 40)? Some find in verse 40, and its reference to 'these my brothers', the suggestion that acts of love for the Jewish people are in view. The words could equally refer to love shown to Jesus' disciples. Or it could be that Jesus identifies himself with all who are hungry, thirsty, sick or in prison, and sees works of love done towards such people as works done to himself. This would be the most inclusive interpretation, excluding none of the other categories. As such, it is the one to prefer, since it poses the greatest challenge to us all. Spontaneous acts of love, generosity and kindness to those in need reveal what is inside us. It is good to do what is good.

Guidelines

Although Jesus portrayed divine judgement in uncompromising and even frightening terms, his message actually belongs to the good news of God's kingdom. A judge is one who presides over a process whereby the truth is allowed to emerge. God's judgement in history is directed towards a final goal when all things will be seen in their true light and then finally put right. The judge of all the earth will do what is just (Genesis 18:25). We await a universal restoration of God's world (Acts 3:21). Victims will be vindicated and perpetrators condemned. Those who long for justice therefore have every reason to place their faith in the God of Jesus Christ and to celebrate the coming of his kingdom. Even more, because the one by whom we shall be judged is Jesus Christ himself (Acts 17:31), we have reason to believe that 'righteousness and peace will kiss each other' in perfect harmony (Psalm 85:10).

What is true on the cosmic level is also true on the personal level. God's judgement is part of God's mercy. It would be an unloving God who allowed us to live in the delusions of sin and spiritual sloth without bringing us to the point of facing up to ourselves. That is what judgement is. We all have elements of spiritual unreality and self-deception residing within us. If we are not prepared to humble ourselves before God, it is not surprising that sometimes God chooses to humble us through events and circumstances (Matthew 23:12). It is better to get our humility in first.

The time when God will resolve the suffering world's injustices is not given us to know. Jesus himself confessed that he knew neither the day nor the hour of his own future coming (24:36). This was one of the many limitations he took on himself in becoming flesh and dwelling among us. The uncertain date of his coming means that every day should be lived in the light of what might be. This is the practical value of not knowing when. Speculation leads nowhere and is, in fact, forbidden in favour of responsible stewardship, living every day in a way that is profitable for ourselves, for others and for God's own self. We are stewards of the gospel of Christ to be invested in people's lives.

1 Love and hatred

Matthew 26:1–16

Here is an incident of intense love sandwiched between two ignoble conspiracies, one between the chief priests and elders (vv. 3–5) and the other between the chief priests and Judas Iscariot (vv. 14–16), both directed against Jesus. The stark contrast is intentional. The unknown woman's demonstration of love for Jesus should be seen in the light of the opening words in verses 1–2: at the Passover feast, Jesus will be handed over to be crucified. The woman anoints his body as an instinctive preparation for his burial and does so out of responsive love (v. 12). By recalling this incident, we fulfil Jesus' prophecy in verse 13, as countless others have done before.

The woman's actions were certainly risky. To anoint a man in this way might have gone beyond the social conventions concerning touch that were acceptable at the time. She was risking her own reputation and perhaps that of Jesus. However, these were small considerations in the face of the momentous events that were unfolding and the need for everyone to make some kind of response to them.

Once more, the disciples come out badly (v. 8). They cannot see beyond the apparent 'waste' involved: the ointment is described as 'very costly'. Judas in particular emerges as a man who knows the price of everything and the value of nothing (vv. 14–15). But Jesus takes the woman's actions as they are intended. These are the last days of his life (v. 11) and the following days will be filled with cruel and very different responses. Opportunities to bless the poor will never be in short supply. Perhaps these are among the last loving, human moments that Jesus will know. Understanding the incident in this way, we can see that the woman has done a fine thing. Perhaps she should be remembered because she has done something for Jesus and something on behalf of us all (v. 13).

If we have love for God, it is because of the prior love of God for us and the fact that he sent his Son as an atoning sacrifice for our sins (1 John 4:10). We do not know which God to love, apart from the one in whom he is revealed. Our hearts are slothful and cannot rise to love unless they are first awakened by the God who, in his Son, draws near.

2 The Last Supper

Elements of the events recorded here have passed into our shared culture, even for those with no understanding of where they come from—especially the idea of 'being a Judas' and the significance of the cockcrow. Also, here we find the foundations of a central Christian practice or sacrament, the sharing of bread and wine in 'Holy Communion' or the 'Lord's Supper'.

As with his entry into Jerusalem, Jesus seems to have made preparation for this occasion (v. 18). It is a mystery to us that although Jesus knew well in advance that Judas would betray him, this did not stop him including the traitor among his closest disciples or breaking bread with him at this meal (v. 23). There is grace here. The sovereign purpose of God was being worked out even through Judas' betrayal—although this did not absolve Judas of responsibility (v. 24).

Judas was not the only disciple to betray Jesus. All the disciples would desert Jesus at the last, and Peter, their leader, would deny him explicitly (vv. 31, 34, 56, 74). They later found repentance, whereas Judas only had remorse. As with them, so with us: there is a large gap between what we think we will do and what we end up doing. All who share in the Lord's Supper are capable of betrayal in their hearts, yet the supper speaks of grace for us also.

An understanding of the cross of Christ as a necessary shedding of his blood for the sake of our forgiveness takes further shape here (v. 28), and will be built upon in the theology of the early church. As the Passover recalled Israel's liberation from bondage in Egypt, so the Lord's Supper reminds us continually of our own liberation from sin and death through Christ's sacrifice. The supper is a modified and extended version of the Passover meal. As Passover recalls the past saving actions of God on behalf of Israel and identifies each new generation within Judaism with the beneficiaries of those acts, so the Lord's Supper reminds us of the cross and resurrection as the work of God for all of us.

Christ has died and Christ has risen (vv. 31–32). But Christ will also come again, so the supper anticipates the heavenly banquet in the kingdom of God and points forward to the time when all shall be well (v. 29).

3 Gethsemane

Even today it is possible to trace the route that Jesus took from inside the city (26:18), down steep steps into the Kidron Valley and then to the garden called Gethsemane, a place seemingly frequented by Jesus and the disciples. The name means 'oil-press' and it is here that Jesus is emotionally and spiritually crushed as he experiences a depth of grief and agitation (v. 37) that we find hard to imagine. His betrayal, arrest, trial and crucifixion are now imminent (v. 47) and events will move forward brutally.

In the garden Jesus undergoes the sense of desolation that will come to its peak on the cross itself (27:46). He communes with his Father (vv. 39, 42) and asks to be released from the trial that awaits him. But something is going on here that simply has to happen. Prophecy has to be fulfilled (v. 56). It is necessary for Jesus to suffer, as has been stated from 16:21 onwards. It involves drinking the cup of suffering, horror and desolation (Ezekiel 23:31–34). The judgement that Israel deserves is now to be freely taken by Jesus upon himself.

Jesus might have walked away from this judgement. A few paces further up the Mount of Olives and he could have disappeared into the Judean desert, never to be seen again. But Jesus chose to undergo this trial, because it was not for himself that he did it but, rather, for us all. The whole story of Matthew's Gospel narrows down to the events of the next few hours: 'I will strike the shepherd, and the sheep of the flock will be scattered' (26:31).

Once more, Jesus' disciples prove to be of little use, failing to support him in his moments of agony (vv. 40, 43, 45), and then scattering when the crowd come to arrest him (v. 56). True to his destined way, Jesus chooses not to resist and enunciates the doctrine that 'all who take the sword will perish by the sword' (v. 52). Refusing to respond to evil by means of evil is part of the meaning of the cross. But how are we to understand the words, 'I will strike the shepherd'? By divine purpose, Jesus is about to stand under judgement and to bear it in our place, the righteous for the unrighteous (1 Peter 3:18).

4 The humiliation of Jesus (and of Peter)

Matthew 26:57–75

Jesus' continues his non-resistance as he is now arraigned before the high priest. These verses breathe authenticity, not just in their description of Jesus but also in the unrelentingly frank way in which they document Peter's abject failure. The passage needs to be read slowly. We may almost feel we are there. Betrayed by his Galilean accent and given the opportunity to be martyred alongside his friend and Lord (26:35), Peter shows himself to be a coward. The cock crows on cue, signifying more than the fact that dawn is breaking. Peter's tears, full of regret and self-loathing, are appropriate. This is not a heroic failure, especially for one who would later lead the church, but Peter represents the other disciples who, unlike him, have by now gone into hiding. He also represents us, and so we have no right to condemn.

Jesus for his part remains silent before his accusers and, in this and many other ways, fulfils the details of that great passage, Isaiah 53, compulsory reading at this point. When compelled to speak, however, he comes as close as anywhere in this Gospel to acknowledging that he is the Messiah and God's Son (vv. 63–64; compare 16:16–17).

The passage makes it clear that Jesus is being unjustly tried (vv. 59–60). Like a lamb, he is being led to the slaughter and taken away by a perversion of justice (Isaiah 53:7–8). The evidence of blasphemy, hard to obtain, consists in a distorted version of what he actually claimed. He knew that the temple would be destroyed but made no claim to destroy it himself, as though he were an insurrectionist. His condemnation is accompanied by the dehumanising and abusive behaviour we have come to expect from unaccountable powers (v. 67). The ugly nature of much that passes as religion, especially religion that has recourse to violence, is revealed here, as it has been revealed many times since. The contrast between the non-violent way of Jesus and the actions of the religious powers should not be missed. Such religion is part of the problem, not of the solution.

Isaiah's great claim was that 'all we like sheep have gone astray; we have all turned to our own way, and the Lord has laid on him the iniquity of us all' (53:6). Here we see it happening.

5 The fate of Judas

It is difficult not to feel sorry for Judas. Having been so close to Jesus and shared in his mission, he has now abandoned any purpose for living. Rarely has anyone been so near, yet so far. Accordingly, Jesus has held out no hope for him (26:24), and in this passage Judas abandons all hope for himself. We have here one of two accounts of his fate, the other being in Acts 1:18–19. We could probably reconcile them, but perhaps it is best simply to let them stand, in all their horror. This is, after all, how they are intended to impact us. To reject the Son of God is no light thing. To turn away from one we have known and loved is unspeakably dangerous.

Inevitably we ask how Judas differs in this respect from Peter and the other disciples, all of whom deserted Jesus at the last. Perhaps there is a difference between failing and rejecting. Failure can be remedied by repentance, but for rejection there can be no forgiveness. Is this a tragic example of 'blasphemy against the Holy Spirit' (12:31)?

If Judas is an example of the corruption of the human heart, then it becomes clear here that sin also has a communal and structural dimension. Establishment religion in the form of the 'chief priests and elders of the people' joins forces with the political power of Pontius Pilate to conspire against Jesus (vv. 1–2). Crucifixion was a form of political punishment, used against any whom the Romans thought were a threat. The prescribed religious punishment for blasphemy was stoning (Acts 7:58–59).

The name of Pilate is recalled every time Christians repeat the Apostles' Creed: Jesus was 'crucified under Pontius Pilate'. It is curious that a corrupt Roman provincial governor should be mentioned in a Christian confession. The reference certainly locates the crucifixion at a certain time in history as an event that indubitably happened. It also serves as a reminder of the inherently unstable nature both of human religion and of human governments. The 'principalities and powers' are fallen and are hard-wired to resist the coming of God's kingdom at all times (Ephesians 6:12). They crucified the Lord of glory (1 Corinthians 2:8). Whatever their usefulness, they need to be regarded with some suspicion and much discernment.

6 Jesus Barabbas or Jesus Christ?

There are those who find this incident hard to credit on historical grounds. They cannot imagine the Romans releasing a 'notorious prisoner' (v. 16) like Barabbas for any reason. Yet strange things do happen. However we assess this opinion, it is widely agreed that the narrative is an outstanding theological statement. Theology is given to us here in pictures rather than propositions, and it will become clear that this is Matthew's preferred method. In short, Barabbas is the first person who is able to say, 'Jesus died in my place', and in his case it is literally true.

There is parallelism here between Jesus Barabbas (literally, 'son of a/ the father') and Jesus the Messiah (v. 17), Son of the Father. The crowds are invited to choose between them, and they choose Barabbas. In so far as anyone has ever deserved to be crucified, it must be Barabbas, whose heinous crimes we can only guess at. By contrast, Jesus is innocent, as Pilate's wife and, by implication, Pilate himself recognise (vv. 19, 23). The innocent one therefore takes the place of the guilty in undergoing condemnation, flogging, mockery and finally death by crucifixion. Jesus is comprehensively rejected (Isaiah 53:3).

We have already noted how a doctrine of atonement has begun to emerge in connection with the cross. Jesus characterised his death as a ransom that had to be paid to set the 'many' free (20:28). At the Last Supper he spoke of his blood as the 'blood of the [new] covenant, which is poured out for many for the forgiveness of sins' (26:28). In Gethsemane he asked that the 'cup' might pass from him but submitted himself to the necessity of doing God's will (26:39, 42). Here we have seen him taking the place of a sinful man as a sign that he is taking the place of all people under divine judgement.

It is not that Jesus himself was judged—he was innocent of all fault and was well pleasing to the Father (3:17). That Jesus himself was being judged by God is unthinkable. Rather, the judgement of others was falling upon him as, at the cross, he displaced us, 'bore the sin of many, and made intercession for the transgressors' (Isaiah 53:12). Like Barabbas, we who are guilty walk away free.

Guidelines

We are now in the very middle of Jesus' ordeal. In the next scenes he will make his way to the cross and be crucified. Despite the horrific nature of crucifixion, neither Matthew nor any other of the Gospel writers attempts to dwell on the details. The facts are recorded soberly and respectfully, with no sensationalism. Unlike Mel Gibson's film *The Passion of the Christ*, the Gospels do not capitalise on the cruelty. This is left to our imagination, and that is enough.

Isaac Watts' great hymn 'When I survey the wondrous cross' is, for most Christians, a masterpiece of devotion. His use of the word 'survey' is particularly significant because it suggests much more than simply looking or gazing at the cross. One who surveys is taking the measure of something, seeking to gauge its height, length and breadth. A surveyor examines a building with care and attention, since much may depend on the accuracy of what he or she does—and this takes time. So it is with the cross of Christ. Its depths are not easily plumbed. We imagine that we have understood what it is all about, only to realise there is more to say, or that what is said might be better expressed. Theories about the meaning of the cross abound and all the metaphors we employ add something to the jigsaw, but we do not have to have a full understanding to enter into its benefits. Here a wonderful exchange has taken place so that what I am has been taken by Christ upon himself and what he is has been given to me, by grace through faith (2 Corinthians 5:21).

No one can be a Christian who does not believe that they need a Saviour. This is a distinguishing mark. It begins with the recognition that we are fallen, spiritually incapable beings who stand no hope of lifting ourselves up to the throne of God. What we need is one who will come to us, engage himself in our plight and triumph over it. This is what we see Jesus doing at the cross. He came to where we are, into the very depths of our lost state, even to the point of death, in order to lift us up and draw us out. He died for us and we died in him.

1 Simon of Cyrene

Matthew 27:32–44

In the soldiers' treatment of Jesus, who has freely made himself vulnerable and helpless, we see some of the worst forms of behaviour of which human beings are capable (27:27–31). The same may be said of those who gathered to watch the spectacle or derided Jesus while he was hanging upon the cross (vv. 39–44).

Golgotha, the 'Place of a Skull' (in Latin known as 'Calvary'), was situated on a slight rise outside the city walls of Jerusalem as they then stood. It was visible from different parts of the city and is reliably identified today by the site of the Church of the Holy Sepulchre.

Jesus had to walk some distance under guard before coming there, carrying the crossbeam to which his arms would be secured before it was hoisted up. A man from Cyrene in Libya was entering the city, possibly a member of the large Jewish community found there and certainly an African. Simon was made to follow Jesus, carrying his cross, and in so doing became a literal picture of discipleship.

When the names of individuals are mentioned in the New Testament, it is usually because they were known in the Christian community and could endorse the account as eyewitnesses. Mark 15:21 further describes Simon as 'the father of Alexander and Rufus', which strongly suggests that both he and his family were part of the early Christian community. A Rufus is also mentioned in Romans 16:13, along with his mother, and this is another probable connection. It seems that the Simon who carried Jesus' cross and followed him went on to do so, along with his family, for the remainder of his life.

These verses contain considerable irony. The charge against Jesus was written above him on the cross and proclaimed him the King of the Jews (v. 37). It was written in mockery, but this does not prevent it from being true. The charge was both religious and political: any claim to kingship would have been a political offence, and the claim to Messiah-kingship would have been offensive to the Jewish authorities. Similarly, the title of Son of God is hurled in Jesus' face (vv. 40, 43). We recall here how reticent Jesus was about claiming to be Messiah or Son of God. Despite this, his friends and enemies alike were in no doubt as to the impact made by his life.

2 The cry of desolation

We now come to Jesus' final moments and the climax of the Gospel. For some time we have been building up to this crisis and especially to the terrible words of verse 46, where Jesus cries out in a loud voice, 'My God, my God, why have your forsaken me?' No wonder Jesus felt crushed and frightened in the garden of Gethsemane, knowing that this ordeal awaited him.

Was he really forsaken by God or was it just that he had journeyed so far into the distant country that he had lost sight of the Father? The answer to the first question could be yes and no: 'For a brief moment I abandoned you, but with great compassion I will gather you' (Isaiah 54:7). In this moment, the Son of God goes into exile on our behalf. He experiences what it means to be lost. He endures what must be the fate of all those who finally reject the source of life: he descends into hell. But he does it all for us, undergoing the fate that we have brought upon ourselves, in order that we do not have to meet it. 'We are convinced that one has died for all; therefore all have died' (2 Corinthians 5:14). The cross therefore becomes a throne of grace where God grants forgiveness to sinners. Forgiveness is bestowed even as sin is atoned for. We can meet him there.

Matthew gives us further theology in pictures. Darkness descends, the earth shakes and the rocks are split, because this is an earth-shattering moment when the Son of God tastes death on our behalf (vv. 45, 51; Hebrews 2:9). The curtain of the temple is torn in two, signifying abundant access to the Father through the sacrifice of Christ. The bodies of Old Testament saints are shaken from their tombs because the death of Christ has opened the gate of life for those who come after him and for the faithful who have gone before.

Were all these real and actual events or are they interpretative windows into the meaning of the greatest of all events? Whichever is the case, there is something in the way Christ dies, yielding up his spirit to God (v. 50), that impresses the centurion in charge and causes him to confess, as have many others, 'Truly this man was God's Son!' (v. 54).

3 Joseph of Arimathea

Matthew 27:55–66

Mary (or Miriam) was a common name for first-century Jewish women. Along with the wealthy Joseph of Arimathea, the women close to Jesus provided not only a compassionate service for him but also an absolutely crucial one. Jewish law required that an executed person's body should be buried on the same day (Deuteronomy 21:22–23). This action was completed by Joseph, a man of some influence and position, who surrendered his own tomb for the purpose. The women noted where that tomb was (v. 61; see also Mark 15:47), with a view to returning after the sabbath. This small detail is greatly significant in the drama that is to follow. Were it not known exactly where Jesus was buried, the empty tomb would not be so significant.

It is entirely understandable human behaviour to want to make sure that a much-loved person, particularly one who has attracted spiritual devotion, is properly buried. This was the case with John the Baptist (14:12) and likewise with Jesus.

Although Jesus had indicated several times to his disciples that he would rise, this was one of many things they appear not to have understood. Ironically, it was Jesus' opponents who remembered it and made attempts to secure the tomb, to ensure that the body was not removed.

We are now being prepared for the great reversal of Jesus' fate that would take place on the third day, with Friday (Preparation Day, v. 62), Saturday and Sunday each being counted as a day. 'Three days' can signify a relatively short period of time, in contrast to '40 days', which is a relatively long period. The calculations are not exact. However, it also has some biblical resonances, as in Hosea 6:2: 'After two days [the Lord] will revive us; on the third day he will restore us, that we may live in his presence' (NIV). The sign of Jonah has already been mentioned in Matthew's Gospel, in 12:40: 'For just as Jonah was for three days and three nights in the belly of the sea monster, so for three days and three nights the Son of Man will be in the heart of the earth.' Here we see that sign being fulfilled as Jesus endures the full impact of death. He was as dead as it is possible to be, thus making the following events even more astonishing.

4 Risen indeed!

Matthew 28:1–10

Matthew chooses to portray the resurrection in the most vivid of terms, with an earthquake, visions of angels, bright lights, trembling and awe. It should be noticed, however, that neither he nor any of the other Gospel writers actually describes the rising of Jesus. It has happened before the morning of the first day of the week and has not been observed by anyone. What is initially unveiled is the empty tomb in which Jesus no longer lies.

This is where it is important to know that the women came to the right tomb. Angels are often introduced into biblical narratives that deal with the presence and power of God. By God's power, Jesus has been raised and the verdict of rejection issued at the cross has been thoroughly overturned. The core of their message is 'He is not here; for he has been raised' (v. 6). It is understandable that the women are filled with mingled fear and joy (v. 8) as they seek to grasp what is taking place. If they are in doubt (for the empty tomb of itself is not enough to prove that Jesus has been raised), such doubt disappears when they encounter Jesus on the way (v. 9). They now worship him.

The first witnesses of the risen Lord are therefore women, a fact that some hold to be highly significant, given that women at the time were not generally regarded as reliable witnesses. Is this a detail that someone would invent, were it not the truth? Not only is it true, but the same women are commissioned as the first evangelists (v. 7). They are to tell the disciples that Jesus will go before them to Galilee, where they will see him. This does indeed happen (see John 21), but they encounter the risen Lord even before that, while they are still in Jerusalem. Perhaps the intention is that in Galilee they will have occasion to come to terms with the fact of the resurrection in familiar territory and to work out its implications.

Matthew only gives us a few scenes in the resurrection narratives; we rely on Luke, John and Paul to give us more. Yet he has already recorded a number of predictions by Jesus of this event, and here those predictions are thoroughly vindicated.

5 Defending the resurrection

No sooner has the resurrection been announced than the claim has to be defended. The most common objection is simply to say that dead people do not rise from the dead. We can only agree. But then, that is the whole point: it is the fact that one person has been uniquely raised that marks him out from all others. Jewish expectation was that there would be a 'general resurrection' in the world to come; the Christian claim is that in Christ the general resurrection has already begun, and that it is the work of God.

The oldest counter-argument to the resurrection is found in these verses. It was an accusation of conspiracy: the disciples had stolen the body and so were claiming falsely that Jesus was alive. This became the standard polemic in the Jewish establishment (v. 15) and, in various forms, has been repeated since that time. The setting of a guard over the tomb is thus seen as a counter-polemic to the claim that the body was removed. How could they remove the body from a guarded tomb (27:66)?

Yet there is a more powerful argument that has never been satisfactorily answered. Why would the disciples invent the resurrection and then be prepared to pay for their deception with their lives? It is against all we know of human nature to suffer and die for something that is known to be untrue. By contrast, however, people can show the most amazing heroism when they are sincerely convinced. And what would convince the first disciples, with all their down-to-earth conditioning as fishermen, tax collectors and the like, other than the presence of an empty tomb and living encounters with the one who had once occupied it (Acts 1:3), now raised into the very life of God?

Objections to the resurrection have become increasingly sophisticated, so the apologetic for it has become both interesting and intellectually rewarding. If we are to be evidence-led, however, the evidence points to its having happened. Evidence to the contrary is meagre and, instead, historical fictions such as the one in this passage are offered. Although it cannot be definitively proved (what ancient historical event can be?), the resurrection can be shown to be the best explanation of the evidence known to us.

6 The great commission

Matthew 28:16–20

As the women were commissioned to tell the good news, so the eleven remaining disciples are now commissioned to take the message to all nations. The Gospel ends on a high point, both literally, since they are on a mountain in Galilee (v. 16), and metaphorically: Jesus has now been given all authority.

Moreover, the theme of inclusion of the Gentiles, which has previously surfaced from time to time, now emerges explicitly as part of the disciples' essential commission. They are to make disciples by seeing people converted to the way of Christ. As the sign that they have joined themselves to the Christian community, these converts are to be baptised in the name of Father, Son and Spirit. They are then to be instructed in the way of Christ by being taught everything that Christ has previously commanded his disciples. The one who is himself called 'God with us' (1:23) promises to continue to be with them to the very end. What is in view here is a large, international, converted, instructed and missionary-hearted community: it is what we know as the Christian Church.

It is striking that the elements of the later Christian doctrine of God can be seen here. There is one name, but that name is Father, Son and Spirit (v. 19): one God with three ways of being God. Unlike in the Gospel of John, this understanding of God has barely surfaced in Matthew's Gospel. It is there in embryo in the baptismal scene (3:16–17) in which the Son is baptised, the Spirit descends upon him and the Father proclaims himself to be well pleased. Likewise, it might be perceived in Jesus' prayer to the Father in 11:25–27, although the Spirit receives no mention there. Undoubtedly, in crafting the words of Jesus in the way he does, Matthew is showing the influence of the early church's developing understanding of the God whose self-revelation unfolds first as Father, then as Son and then as Spirit. He also reveals the importance that the early church laid upon baptism as the way of signifying that a person had passed from spiritual death into life.

The good news of Christ, so brilliantly outlined in this Gospel as a whole, needs to be shared, and nobody should be excluded from hearing it.

Guidelines

In his monumental book *A History of Christianity: The first three thousand years* (Penguin, 2010), the historian Diarmaid MacCulloch begins by quoting the final verse from Samuel Crossman's seasonal hymn, 'My song is love unknown':

Here might I stay and sing,
No story so divine,
Never was love, dear King!
Never was grief like Thine.
This is my Friend,
In Whose sweet praise
I all my days
Could gladly spend.

He then goes on to assert, as he also does in the accompanying BBC TV series, that Christianity is at root a 'personality cult'.

Its central message is the story of a person, Jesus, whom Christians believe is also the Christ (from a Greek word meaning 'Anointed One'): an aspect of the God who was, is and ever shall be, yet who is at the same time a human being, set in historic time. (p. 1)

Now, granted that we are more likely to associate the term 'personality cult' either with Stalin's Russia or North Korea's 'dear leader' Kim Jong-un, Mac-Culloch is surely right (though the word 'cult' is unattractive). Christianity's magnificent obsession is with the life, death, resurrection and continuing vitality of Jesus Christ. As MacCulloch goes on to say:

Christians believe that they can still meet this human being in a fashion comparable to the experience of the disciples who walked with him in Galilee and saw him die on the Cross. They are convinced that this meeting transforms lives, as has been evident in the experience of other Christians across the centuries.

A personality cult indeed, but one that follows the subversive logic that Jesus himself employed when he declared in Matthew 23:9, 'And call no one your father on earth, for you have one Father—the one in heaven.' So, for Christians, Jesus is the only personality who finally matters, and he abolishes any other kind of cult, personality or otherwise, that might be invented on earth. Jesus is one of the most compelling and attractive personalities ever to have lived, and being his disciple consists both in seeking to follow in his footsteps and in telling his story to one and all. Matthew's Gospel portrays Jesus as the new Moses, and contains all the instruction we need to continue in his way. It also assures us that he continues with us—to the end of the age (28:20).

FURTHER READING

Matthew Black and H.H. Rowley, *Peake's Commentary on the Bible*, Thomas Nelson, 1963.

Amy-Jill Levine and Marc Zvi Brettler, *The Jewish Annotated New Testament*, Oxford University Press, 2011.

Leon Morris, *The Gospel According to Matthew*, IVP, 1992.

Tom Wright, *Matthew for Everyone Part 1 (Chapters 1—15)* and *Part 2 (Chapters 16—28)*, SPCK, 2002.

The journey of leadership in the life of Moses

Moses is the preeminent figure in the Old Testament. He receives the law from God at Mount Sinai and guides the Israelites from Egypt to the promised land. He is the only person who speaks to God 'face to face', and we might be tempted to portray him as a faultless, heroic figure of faith. Yet the biblical depiction of Moses is far from that of an idealised saint.

Moses experiences many victories in his leadership but he also suffers numerous failures, jeopardising God's plan of salvation for his people and for the whole earth. Yet there is good reason to understand Moses as the archetypal leader, despite his apparent lack of 'success'. Where Moses fails in the eyes of the world, he succeeds in the eyes of God. He is the first great suffering servant of the Bible who lays down his life for his sheep, and it is through his example that we can learn what God values in leadership.

Scholars are generally agreed that the text of the book of Exodus is composite in form and has been shaped over the centuries to bring together the dramatic salvation history of Israel through the deliverance from Egypt, the wilderness wanderings, the covenant at Sinai and the building of the tabernacle. Although much fruitful work can be done in discerning the different sources behind the narratives, in the following studies we will consider the text in its final form. It is likely that the priestly authors/redactors brought together Exodus during the Babylonian exile, so we will approach the text following the narrative that they have created. In this way we will explore the life of Moses as it is presented in the story of Exodus and the theological implications that arise from witnessing his growth as the first great leader and shepherd of God's people.

Quotations are taken from the New Revised Standard Version of the Bible.

1 A heart for justice

Exodus 2:11–25

Our introduction to the adult Moses comes amid the unjust structures of the Egyptian kingdom. The regime of Pharaoh has been merciless to the Israelite slaves. Until this point in the story, we have only witnessed the non-violent, passive resistance of the midwives (1:17). Their brave opposition spares the lives of innocent children and undermines Pharaoh's plan of exterminating the Israelite boys. It is against this backdrop that we come to Moses' first response to injustice.

It has often been noted that Moses' actions in 'seeing' and 'striking' the Egyptian man foreshadow what God will eventually do to Pharaoh and Egypt, but the difference between Moses' and God's acts is significant for our understanding of appropriate responses to oppression. Moses responds to brute violence with violence, and he completely fails. He mistakes vigilantism as an appropriate response to injustice and responds to the cry of the oppressed out of his own strength, without the authority of the community, the law or the command of God.

In spite of his error, however, we see that Moses has a passion for justice and a sense of the value of human life. He perceives in his heart the moral design of creation and recognises the need to defend the poor and oppressed. This is what we find in the next section of the passage, after Moses has escaped to Midian. He defends the priest's daughters by driving off the shepherds who have treated them unfairly, and this time he succeeds without having to kill or flee for his life (vv. 16–17).

These two stories of Moses' early life in Egypt and Midian seem to be placed side by side for a reason. Together they demonstrate that Moses shares God's passion for justice and care for the poor and oppressed. As a leader called by God, he must maintain the desire to bring justice to those who suffer but he also must also learn to listen and to act in God's time. In the final verses of the chapter, we have a succession of verbs that describe God's response to the Israelites' cry: God *heard*, God *remembered*, God *looked upon*, and God *took notice*. God will act on behalf of his people in a way never seen before, to bring them justice, and he chooses Moses as a leader because Moses shares this passion.

2 A shepherd for God's people

It is often the case in the Bible that God calls people in weakness and in moments of despair to take leadership roles in his kingdom. In many ways, Moses sets this pattern for future prophets and disciples through his own experience. He has fallen from the heights of the Egyptian royal courts and has fled to the land of Midian, which lies just east of the Sinai Peninsula in modern-day Saudi Arabia. There he becomes a shepherd and tends the flocks of his father-in-law, Jethro (v. 1).

It is significant that Moses goes from eating and drinking with royalty to tending sheep as part of his preparation to lead Israel. He has been stripped of his former worth and significance and now must find his identity among the flocks. Though a humble position in ancient society, the role of the shepherd was to protect, feed and nurture sheep that were often exposed to danger. Good shepherds risked their lives to protect their flocks, even if it was from purely financial motivation.

Beyond the practical concerns of protecting his livelihood, a good shepherd needed to be fully committed to the preservation and care of the flock, which is why ancient gods and kings often assumed this title, marking them out as caretakers of their people. The great Babylonian king Hammurabi was known as a shepherd. The Babylonian god Marduk was called a faithful shepherd, and even the Egyptian Pharaoh Amenhotep III was called the good shepherd. God, too, claims this title in dramatic fashion when he condemns the priests and leaders of Israel through the prophet Ezekiel, before the Babylonian exile (Ezekiel 34:15–16).

Moses is not called to lead God's people because of his eloquence, his brilliant mind or his rugged good looks. Instead, he is called because he has a shepherd's heart and is prepared to lead God's people in the unglamorous work of seeking out lost sheep, binding their wounds and taking them to pasture where they might grow and thrive. Moses must first learn to love his flock in the isolation of the wilderness, where there is no one to praise his sacrificial acts or to laud his selfless work. This is the biblical proving ground for those who will lead and lay down their lives for God's people, in the same manner as God himself.

3 What's in a name?

Having seen the awesome sight of the burning bush, and having been invited to stand on holy ground, Moses receives his call into God's plan of redemption and salvation for Israel and for the world. For the one who previously wanted to bring justice to his people in Egypt, this seems like the opportune time to accept God's command. Yet, unlike the courageous heroes of ancient epics, Moses cowers, questions and ultimately rejects God's request. A fine way for the greatest figure of the Old Testament to start out!

With the call to leadership and the promise of divine presence comes the revelation of God's name. This consists of four Hebrew consonants, YHWH, known as the tetragrammaton. It is often pronounced 'Yahweh' in contemporary English but remains unpronounced by Jews, who often substitute the word Adonai ('Lord'). Why was the name so important? Knowing a god's name in the ancient world was often associated with having certain magical powers over that god, because you could call upon it in times of need. Yet the name that God reveals here is far from clear. It is the present or future form of the verb 'to be' and so could be translated 'I Am who I Am' or 'I Will Be who I Will Be'. The obscurity of the name has generated much debate about whether it refers to God's eternal essence or his unchangeable being. What the name does convey, however, is the sense that God, as 'I Am' or 'I Will Be', is someone who cannot be defined but will reveal himself throughout history. Thus the name is ever pregnant with potential: God is always present to give birth to new revelation as he calls us to follow him faithfully.

This is what Moses will experience throughout his life as leader of Israel. He will embark on an ever-deepening journey into the heart of God as he suffers and sacrifices his life on behalf of Israel. The revelation of the divine name reminds us that a call to leadership in God's kingdom is not without the promise of his presence and the promise that he will always open up to us a new revelation of his glory and salvation.

4 Refusing the call

Exodus 4:1–17; 6:2–13

Many biblical stories are very refreshing because they are very real. Moses is afraid, and we would be too. Yet Moses' fear is not only of Pharaoh; it is also the fear of being rejected by his own people. These are the two fears that stand in any leader's way—fear of those on the outside and fear of those on the inside.

The detail and length of Moses' dialogue with God is unprecedented in the Bible and is not found in any other call narrative. It's as if the biblical authors want us to understand that this was no easy choice and that God does not force anyone into leadership. The conversation reveals Moses' increasing anxiety about his calling, and yet God does not bully him into submission. Instead he lures, invites, entices, listens, accommodates and encourages. As Jeremiah will later say of his own calling, 'O Lord, you have enticed me, and I was enticed' (Jeremiah 20:7).

It is a risky thing for God to entrust his works into the hands of human beings, but, because he does, he opens up a path for fuller revelation whereby human interaction creates new possibilities for the unfolding of the divine will. What is so critical throughout Moses' life, as he leads and intercedes for Israel, is that he is no puppet on a string, simply accepting what God commands. Rather, he questions, pleads and offers prayers on behalf of God's people, and God responds. The Lord does not call his children to become his robots but, instead, invites us to enter more deeply into relationship with him, where our own passions can grow and be expressed as we lead others.

At the heart of biblical leadership is relationship. Although God calls Moses into his plan of salvation for Israel, he is, more importantly, calling him into relationship. It is remarkable that toward the end of the conversation Moses exclaims, 'O my Lord, please send someone else!' (4:13). Yet God, in spite of his anger, changes his plan for his servant and allows Aaron to participate. Why doesn't God just give up on Moses at this point? Because he is 'merciful and gracious, slow to anger, and abounding in steadfast love and faithfulness' (Exodus 34:6). In his patience he takes the raw material of each one of us and begins his work of transformation as he draws us further and further into his presence.

5 Going from bad to worse

There is no guarantee of worldly success when we are called to lead in God's kingdom. In fact, when the apostle Paul wrote to the new Christians in Philippi, he often used the word 'suffer' to define his life in Christ, and encouraged them to suffer for Christ's sake (Philippians 1:29). Moses also found himself suffering for God after heeding the call to deliver Israel from slavery in Egypt. After the revelation of the burning bush and having gained the support of the Israelites, Moses and Aaron confront Pharaoh with God's message. They have obeyed God's call and now it is up to him to live up to his of the bargain. Instead of victory and celebration, however, the suffering of the Israelites only increases. What happened?

Some commentators note that Moses does not do exactly as the Lord has commanded him. He does not perform the signs God has given him (4:21) and, instead, resorts to plea-bargaining with Pharaoh. Whether it is due to Moses' disobedience or God's purposeful delay is debatable, but the narrative builds in tension and Moses' leadership is tested in the face of immeasurable challenges. Pharaoh is against him and even the people whom he longs to save despise him. How do biblical leaders respond in such dire circumstances? They pray.

Prayer will become a theme of Moses' leadership when he faces insurmountable obstacles. He recognises his own weakness and inability to rectify the situation, but he also remembers God's role. He blames God for not acting according to his promise and then turns his focus toward himself, asking, 'Why did you ever send me?' (vv. 22–23). The feeling of failure and rejection reveals an important cry of those who are called into God's service. It is a cry emerging from faithful obedience which suffers rejection from both the world and the people entrusted to our care. It is a cry heard even on the lips of the Son of God upon the cross: 'My God, my God, why have you forsaken me?' (Matthew 27:46).

The voice of God's leaders and prophets is often rejected because it goes out to a world that has gone numb to his goodness. Yet Moses' prayer does not go unheard; it is through prayer and suffering that he will help to bring about the salvation of God's people.

6 Victory at the Sea of Reeds

Exodus 15:1–19

The first great climax of Exodus takes place at the crossing of the Sea of Reeds (often called the 'Red Sea' in English Bibles, a name that comes from an early mistranslation of the Hebrew into Greek). It is here that God strikes his decisive blow against Egypt and the Israelites are finally set free. After all the hardship and more than 400 years of slavery, Moses celebrates through song.

The song of Moses is thought to be one of the oldest hymns contained in the Bible. It celebrates the victory of God over Pharaoh and over the cosmic forces that brought oppression and slavery to his people. In many ways it acts as a psalm of praise, providing an exclamation mark after 14 chapters of lament in Egypt. Although the militaristic images (such as 'the Lord is a warrior', v. 3) might not sit well with contemporary readers, the thrust of the song is that Yahweh is the God who is present and powerful to save.

Moses' song reminds us that there are times when we should sing and shout for joy at what the Lord has done among us. It is right to recall and to celebrate the great things God has done because it leads to faith and trust, it passes on praise from one generation to the next, and it reminds the community of faith that God is living and active among his people. This God is not far off, high in the heavens; he is present and is bringing about the redemption of the world through his people.

We are not told that Moses ever sang again. In Deuteronomy 31:30—32:43, he speaks the words of the song that God has commanded him to write (31:19), but he does not sing. It is a sober reminder that leading and shepherding God's people is no easy task and often comes with much suffering. There is also joy, however. The praise of God should be sung among the community of faith as an ever-present reminder that Yahweh is a God who delivers from slavery and death by his mighty works and leads his people into new life.

Guidelines

The beginning of Moses' life offers us important insights into what it means to lead in God's kingdom. The flawed character of Moses reminds us that leadership in God's kingdom is not about being strong or without fault, but is about sharing in the passions of God's heart. Do we fear God's call in our lives? That's fine; so did Moses. Do we make terrible mistakes? Don't worry; so did Moses. There are two most important questions. Are we willing to love and sacrifice our lives for others? And are we willing to draw near to God's heart so that he might transform our own hearts? This is what Moses did best.

Two things about biblical leadership stand out in these early chapters of Exodus—Moses' passion for justice and his shepherd's heart. Despite all his weaknesses and insecurities, he shares God's desire for justice and mercy for the poor and oppressed. He is also committed to the care, love and sacrifice of a shepherd. This is a poignant reminder for us as Christians that God calls each of us to establish his justice in the world and to love his people. In doing this, we too will feed God's sheep and sustain his flock.

The first part of Moses' life story ends with a victory and a song at the sea. Singing and rejoicing are central to the Christian life. When was the last time we really celebrated with others in remembrance of all that God has done? When, as leaders, have we stood up in the congregation to remind everyone of what God has done? The life of the body of Christ is always strengthened when we celebrate God's works together and witness to what he is doing in our midst. So let us remember that, as we take on leadership roles in the church or in our local communities, we don't need to be great, but we do need a shepherd's heart to love God's people, to lay down our lives for others, and to bring justice and mercy to those in need.

1 Manna and rest for the people

Exodus 16

After one of the greatest victories in the Bible, at the Sea of Reeds, Moses' leadership is immediately challenged in the wilderness, and so begins the rollercoaster ride for the shepherd of God's people. Instead of praise and recognition for all his efforts, Moses gets mumbling and complaints.

The wilderness is a liminal place where Moses and the Israelites will wander for 40 years. There is no life, no fertility, and no land of milk and honey. The desert is a place of testing, where the Lord wants to form a people in holiness before they enter the land of Canaan. There are times in our lives when we too must lead people through such barren places, and it requires patience, love and faithfulness. It is apparent from the story of the manna and quail that Moses calls the people to 'draw near to the Lord' (v. 9) because God will provide. As the shepherd of Israel, Moses understands that he can only offer so much, but he *can* direct his people to the great shepherd who provides. We may often be able to offer physical, emotional or spiritual help to others, but ultimately our job as leaders is to bring people to Christ, where they may feed on the bread of life and drink from his living waters (John 6:35; 7:37–38).

The message of this passage is that the Lord is a God who provides and meets the needs of his children. Though the Israelites grumble, God responds in mercy, and he also teaches them a valuable lesson that will form the core life pattern of this holy people. God's children need rest. They need a sabbath day to cease from the toil of their work so that they may reflect, praise, worship, enjoy family and community, and be thankful. Moses must establish this pattern in his own life too, and it is a pattern that must be set by those leading in the church today. It is critical that, as we lead, we set an example of rest for those around us. This doesn't mean being legalistic about Sundays, but it does require us to know the sabbath rest of Christ in our own lives so that we might model it and share it with others.

2 Water in the wilderness

Exodus 17:1–7; Numbers 20:1–13

Good shepherds provide water for their flocks, and so good leaders provide refreshment for those whom they lead. But providing refreshment and life-giving waters isn't always easy, especially when the people you're leading want to stone you (17:4)!

The place names given by Moses in this story come from two Hebrew verbs—*massah*, which means 'to test', and *meribah*, which means 'to strive, contend', carrying the sense of a legal dispute. The Israelites have placed Moses and God on trial over a lack of water, and Moses once again turns to the Lord in prayer and asks, 'What shall I do?'

The instructions are simple: use the staff that you've used before and strike the rock. At this point, God allows Moses to use the tools that have been familiar to him in his leadership of the people thus far. In Numbers

20, however, after the revelation and giving of the law at Mt Sinai, we find a similar passage where the command is slightly different.

Moses has seen the Lord face to face, he has come down from Sinai radiant with God's glory (Exodus 34:4–5, 29), and now, as Israel strives with him once more, he is told to speak to the rock so that it will produce water. God's command echoes the very act of creation, in which he speaks and the natural world responds. God is stretching Moses in his leadership. Moses doesn't need to rely on his old staff but is encouraged to speak the word that will provide refreshment for his people. The Lord also uses this moment of conflict to draw Moses into a more intimate relationship, if he trusts and responds in obedience. Unfortunately, Moses doesn't listen but goes back to his old staff and strikes the rock twice (Numbers 20:11). The effect is the same as before—water comes out—but he has missed an opportunity for growth and will never enter the promised land.

It is tempting, as leaders, to fall back on what has worked for us in the past, but God is always calling us to experience him anew. It is easy to get stuck in patterns that produce good results, but we are called to so much more in his kingdom. God's desire is that we seek him first and, like Moses, fall on our knees in prayer—to listen so that he might draw us further into relationship and provide refreshment for his people through us.

3 The calling of a priestly and holy people

Exodus 19:1–25

Many scholars consider the giving of Torah (a word often translated 'law' but, more accurately, meaning 'teaching') at Sinai as the second major climax of Exodus after the deliverance at the Sea of Reeds. Time seems to slow down in the biblical narrative at this point, and the Israelites will not leave Sinai until Numbers 10. Yet this is no ordinary stop along the way; the covenant at Sinai provides the defining relationship and identity of God's people before they enter the promised land.

The scene at Sinai is somewhat terrifying as God descends on the mountain in a thick cloud with thunder, lightning, fire and smoke. The revelation highlights the holiness of God and the way Israel might approach him, foreshadowing the delineations of holiness in the tabernacle and temple. These divisions of holiness, however, must be understood within the context of Israel's calling.

As the Israelites enter into covenant, they are called to be a 'priestly kingdom and a holy nation' (v. 6). Here we find a 'democratisation' of holiness, whereby every Israelite is called to be set apart and to act as a priest. But why have a kingdom of priests if Israel has other priests that serve in the temple? The priestly calling is one of intercession. Priests in all ancient religions acted as mediators between God and humanity, through prayers, offerings and sacrifices. Thus the whole of Israel, as God's chosen ones, are to be like a nation of priests, offering intercession on behalf of the world. The Torah given through Moses will be their guide on how to live as a holy nation of priests for the blessing of all the nations (Genesis 12:2–3).

The apostle Peter uses this very language as he assures the Gentiles that they too have become 'a royal priesthood, a holy nation' in Christ (1 Peter 2:9–10). The calling of Israel is no less the calling of the Church—to be a priestly people of intercession on behalf of the world. Although there are still priests and pastors who lead in the church, the covenant in Christ requires all to strive for holiness and to live out the priestly role of intercessor. In God's economy, all people are leaders in his kingdom and, although some have different roles in the community of faith, all are called to holiness and a priestly life.

4 Leading through crisis: the golden calf

Exodus 32:1–14

The goal of Moses' leadership was to set free an oppressed people and guide them to the promised land. To become God's chosen people, however, Israel must enter into a covenant relationship with the God who has delivered them from slavery. A covenant was a type of legal contract in the ancient world, often made between a suzerain and a vassal, or a king and his servant. Once the stipulations of the covenant had been broken, the contract was void and a new covenant would have to be made.

The sin of the golden calf might be seen as the most serious in the Old Testament. This is no minor infringement but an outright rejection of God's plan of salvation for Israel and for the whole world. By their sin the Israelites have broken the covenant, and we are left asking, 'How can an unholy people remain in covenant with a holy God?' This is the question that underlies the entire Old Testament and is ultimately answered in the once-for-all sacrifice of Christ. Before Jesus comes, however, what will Moses (and other prophets/leaders) do to maintain Israel's relationship with a holy God?

The Israelites are in need of an intercessor, and Moses stands in the gap to plead on behalf of the sheep he loves. It is interesting that God asks Moses to leave him alone (v. 10), when God can do as he pleases. This brief pause, however, invites Moses to respond, and he does so by appealing to God's patience, his reputation and his promise to the patriarchs. The Lord listens and relents from bringing destruction.

Moses, as the archetypal leader of Israel, sets the pattern for the one who lays down his life for his sheep and pleads on their behalf. The author of Hebrews tells us that Jesus did the same: 'In the days of his flesh, Jesus offered up prayers and supplications, with loud cries and tears, to the one who was able to save him from death, and he was heard because of his reverent submission' (Hebrews 5:7). And Jesus continues to intercede for us today (Hebrews 7:25).

Are we willing to lay down our lives for the sheep that have been entrusted to us? Are we willing to plead for them and stand in the gap on their behalf? And do we believe that God will hear our prayers and respond? This is the calling of a biblical leader.

5 Seeing God face to face

Exodus 33:1–18

The destruction of Israel having been averted, God explains to Moses that he cannot go with the people into the land, lest he consume them, and so he will send an angel to guide them instead (vv. 2–3). The great covenant that would have allowed a holy God to dwell in the midst of Israel has been broken, and the people rightfully mourn.

There are times when all seems lost as we try to shepherd God's people. Yet, in this moment of desperation, Moses once again falls on his knees to pray. This time, however, we have a different description of what happens at the 'tent of meeting'. The tent is outside the camp because God cannot be in their midst, and it is Moses who initiates the conversation. God responds by descending and then speaks with Moses 'face to face, as one speaks to a friend' (v. 11). What is so outstanding about this passage is not only Moses' intimacy with God but also the fact that the God of the heavens listens and responds to the call of his children. This is the God who is accessible to his children and wants to meet with them face to face when they call on him.

We might wonder why, after an experience of such intimacy, Moses prays, 'Show me your glory' (v. 18). How can he become more intimate with God? Here we find one of the mysteries of prayer: the more we experience God's presence, the greater will be our desire to know him. Moses longs to be in deeper communion with God and to know him, but he discovers, more significantly, that *he* is known by God and is God's beloved (v. 17). It is out of this intimacy and understanding of God that Moses can continue in his leadership of the people.

The goal of leadership in the Bible is not so much about what we do as about who we become. God gave Moses a shepherd's heart but Moses needed to grow into his calling through prayer, struggle and intimate communion with God. The more Moses comes to know God's heart and love for his people, the more he is transformed into God's image and reflects that love to the Israelites.

6 Abiding in glory

Exodus 33:19—34:10

God responds to Moses' request by saying that no one can see his face and live. The biblical authors were well aware that, just a few verses earlier, God has spoken to Moses 'face to face'. So how do we reconcile such a blatant contradiction? The request to see God's 'glory' seems to indicate something beyond normal prayer. Moses is asking for a full revelation of the almighty God who is wholly other. How can anyone know or see such a revelation? It is impossible, and so God concedes that Moses can see his 'back', as if catching a glimpse of a king's majestic train.

God's agreement to pass by Moses and reveal his glory acts as a form of covenant renewal. God will mend what has been broken by the Israelites and, in doing so, will reveal his character. When the Lord speaks, we hear one of the foundational statements of who God is, which echoes throughout the Old Testament. The God who will renew the covenant with Israel is a God who is 'merciful', a word that in Hebrew is closely related to 'womb' and expresses a mother's tender love for her child. He is also 'gracious', 'slow to anger' and 'abounding in steadfast love'. He forgives sin; he is also just, but will not let iniquity be passed on further than to the fourth generation. Moses wants to 'know' God and to see his glory, and this is what God reveals.

The experience of the divine presence gives birth to theological knowledge. Moses now knows the defining character of God, which is critical as he intercedes for the Israelites. He understands that the covenant will ultimately be upheld by divine mercy, and this will guide his future prayers.

Leadership in the Bible is defined by the way we understand and experience the living God. The further Moses is drawn into the divine presence, the more he becomes like the great shepherd. God's desire is to reveal his glory so that the more we come to know him and experience his presence through the Holy Spirit, the more we understand what it means to lead and care for his people.

Guidelines

Moses is a leader unlike any other in the Old Testament. Although he guides the Israelites from Egypt to the edge of the promised land, it is his relationship with God that stands out. His life is a testimony to the centrality of prayer and how, through prayer and obedience, he participates in God's own glory (Exodus 34:29). No one else will experience such a thing until the Son of God is transfigured on the mountain top (Matthew 17:1–5).

The apostle Paul says that this glory is passed on to us as we are changed in Christ (2 Corinthians 3:7–18). As bearers of Christ's glory, we are all called into leadership roles within God's kingdom and within the church as we follow in the steps of great leaders like Moses.

How, then, can we become like Moses? The first question we might ask is: do I love my sheep? In other words, do I love those whom God has placed in my life to care for and to guide? We might also examine our prayer life. Do we pray to seek God's guidance, especially when there is conflict? Is our leadership rooted in a life of prayer? And finally, how are we growing in intimacy in our own relationship with Christ? Sometimes it can be easier to help others grow than to take care of our own faith, but Moses demonstrates that we lead best when our lives are firmly rooted in God's presence.

FURTHER READING

Brevard S. Childs, *The Book of Exodus: A critical, theological commentary*, Westminster, 1974.

Terence E. Fretheim, *Exodus*, John Knox, 1991.

Moshe Greenberg, *Understanding Exodus*, Behrman House, 1969.

Nahum M. Sarna, *Exploring Exodus: The heritage of biblical Israel*, Schocken, 1986.

Numbers

Numbers may not be top of your list if you are looking for inspiration but it shouldn't be overlooked. If 'all scripture is inspired by God' (2 Timothy 3:16) then Numbers may have something special to offer about community and relationships.

'Numbers' is simply the title given by the translators, presumably because the book begins with a census, but it is not about 'numbers' and certainly not statistics. It is about people: it tells of a community on a journey from slavery to freedom. The Hebrew title, 'In the Wilderness', is more apt because that is a journey we are all familiar with. 'Wilderness' is a significant experience for most communities at some point or other. The details may vary but the similarities are remarkable. So, as you read, reflect and pray, think about steps on the journey of life.

The opening chapters read almost like a shopping list of not very meaningful items, but they are the key to the community. They describe the fairly natural response of people to the problems they encounter, and the highs and lows of the leadership. So who are these people and where are they coming from?

Popularly known as 'the Israelites', their tribal names define them as descendants of Jacob, but Jacob lived anything up to 500 years earlier. Over time, Joseph's privileged position at the Egyptian court had become history, and his descendants found themselves slaves, until they escaped under the leadership of Moses.

When we get to Numbers, we find a mixed community, several hundreds if not thousands (the figures are suspect because the wilderness could never have supported a community of that size), escaping from persecution. Anything, even wilderness, is better than torture, but it isn't long before the thrill of freedom gives way to frustration and anxiety which are not satisfied by wandering.

There comes a point where they have no idea where they are going, or whether they are going anywhere except round in circles. The future looks very much like the past, with no sign of an end. To make matters worse, the community and leaders are losing any sense of cohesion. Someone needs to take control. A direction has to be set. How do people and leaders respond in a time of crisis, and with what consequences? By the end of our fortnight's studies, if we find ourselves more in our world than in theirs, that could be because we seek to worship the same God, with a similar vision, facing similar challenges.

Quotations are taken from the New Revised Standard Version.

1 The building of community

Numbers 1:1–4, 16–19

These verses are a kind of plan for the next five chapters. The details matter little but the underlying principles are fundamental for any society. They say something important about transforming a rabble into a structured community, by a method which the Israelites believed was as God would wish it to be. This is not to suggest that we should copy the details; rather, we can see the principles as a litmus test for any community which claims to be founded on the Judeo-Christian tradition—we might almost say, contemporary Western society. There are five steps.

- First, if they are to fulfil their desire for unity and cooperation, they need to know who they are and to recognise their near neighbours.
- Second, they need security, not necessarily within their community but as they travel together through rough and unknown territory. That means identifying men over 20 with a capacity to defend everyone when necessary.
- Third, they need mature men (and, in this world, men it had to be) who can exercise overall care and responsibility for maintaining the rules, regulations and ethos of the society. Since these men have to be impartial, they are to be identified from the start as 'different'; hence the special role of the Levites.
- Fourth, every tribe needs to know its place in the overall scheme of things. There was a pecking order when the whole Israelite community came to move. Each tribe had its own space and place; we might wonder if the planners thought about which tribes could live cheek by jowl and which needed to be kept at a distance.

- Fifth, they need a focal point as a marker, equally accessible to all. For the Israelites, this was the ark of the covenant, the symbol of Yahweh and all that he meant to them.

Success depended on strong leadership. It was a plus that they all shared a common heritage over several hundred years. A minus was that, during those years, each tribe had developed its own customs and traditions; sometimes, being similar but different can be more demanding than being wholly other.

2 Two tests of nonconformity

Numbers 6:1–12, 21–26

Every community has its nonconformists, and needs them, even if at times they appear to be little more than misfits or irritants. The Nazirites, something of an uncertain quantity, may come into this category.

The Hebrew *nazar* suggests separation, with Joseph, who was 'set apart from his brothers', as one of the early contenders for the title (Genesis 49:26). An alternative interpretation relates these people to the Hebrew *nezer* (meaning a 'vow') because they took a vow and thereby separated themselves from the rest. Whether the vow was temporary or permanent, and whether Nazirite identity changed over the 1000 years of Old Testament history, is uncertain. It probably did change, but at this point it is clear that they were intended to separate themselves from others by abstinence from wine, unshorn hair and avoidance of anything that might make them ritually unclean. Such finer points are for scholars. What matters more to us is two tests of nonconformity.

First, the Nazirites stand out from the rest: the rest know this, recognise them, respect them and accept them for what they are, not what many would like them to be—geniuses, eccentrics or just plain 'oddities'. The Nazirites don't expect anyone to join them, never give the impression that their way is the only way, and show no evidence that they see themselves as superior.

Second, Nazirites who make a vow (Deuteronomy 23:21–23) are expected to live up to what they proclaim. They are neither ardent environmentalists who busy themselves flying from one international conference to another nor voluble pacifists who have a reputation for 'upping the ante' when suddenly threatened in their own home. A good Nazirite is one who chooses to make a vow and keeps it. A bad Nazirite is one who makes a vow and breaks it. If you are tempted to identify 'Nazirites' of your acquaintance, to see which side of that line they are on, it's best first to take a look in a mirror.

Those who pass the test are worthy to receive the priestly benediction.

3 The stabilisers

Numbers 9:9–23

Every community needs its stabilisers—people who, whether natives or resident aliens, can live as God intended, one sign of which is to identify with the community by sharing appropriately in the traditional customs and traditions. This is not for the benefit of the stabilisers but for the health of the community, because the stabilisers are the people who keep the community safe, steady and pointing in the right direction.

One aspect of this function is to show respect for, and to retain, the things that really matter—in the Israelites' case, the Passover. Two rules are paramount. First, those who think that their way of life has prohibited them from participation (they have offended in some way or other and feel excluded, or they know that they do not naturally belong) are reassured that they are part of the whole. Second, those who just cannot be bothered are dismissed as having excluded themselves.

So the strength of a community depends on those who are prepared to commit themselves to involvement, 'both the resident alien and the native' (v. 14), rather than on those who claim involvement as a right (even a privilege) but will not lift a finger to show their commitment.

Another important point is to know when to move and when to stick. The Israelites' dependence on the cloud for guidance (v. 17) may seem somewhat primitive and unreliable for 21st century scientific creatures, but is it something we ought to examine more seriously? Could it be simply a matter of relating more closely to nature? Who would want to move into unfamiliar territory when the weather is mirky and potentially dangerous? In a prescientific society, it would be natural to attribute anything you didn't quite understand to God. Were these people early environmentalists? Like the swallow (Jeremiah 8:7), other migratory birds, and animals which produce their young only when there is likely to be food, they knew their appointed time. Theologically, in a world where nature works in harmony with God, the Israelites may well have understood the weather and the environment as God's messengers. Get it right and there will be food ahead. Get it wrong and you may thirst or starve or catch disease. A successful community needs people with that kind of wisdom.

4 When the wheels come off

Numbers 11:1–15

The Beatles, 1965. 'Yesterday, all my troubles seemed so far away.' It was a catchy melody with sentiments that resonated, even more than the tune, with many people. At this stage in their journey, the Israelites would have loved it. But how were they to get from yesterday to today, and then to tomorrow?

Step 1 on the road to 'yesterday' is dissatisfaction with today. Nobody hankers after the past if the present is good and the future holds hope. Why would they? Everything the Israelites remember was dreadful. Today is not like that. Their escape was exhilarating. Crossing the Jordan was like tearing down a huge dividing wall. The troubles to come will be 'challenging', but they have a big heart and a good leader. But now, today… the wheels are coming off. Hopes are not simply unrealised; they are being dashed. And when that happens, Step 2 kicks in.

Obedience gives way to murmuring and rebellion. The people hark back to when meat was plentiful, fish was cheap and vegetables varied. Now there is nothing but manna, discoloured and tasteless, day after day. It's easy for us to be critical, but harder to remember the similar cry of the European war-weary nations who endured the stringency of rationing in World War II. Many contemporary voices bemoan the loss of local products, locally available from small traders, rather than fast food, packaged and processed.

No wonder Moses is 'displeased', but why is Yahweh 'angry' (v. 10)? Because they are turning up their noses at what he offers, or because his people seem to have forgotten why they are in the place where they are? Nobody drove them into the wilderness. This was what they wanted. Any sacrifice was worth making in exchange for freedom. But now is the time to accept responsibility for what is past and tackle the new situation in which they find themselves. The need is to get from yesterday to today and tomorrow.

Of course we sympathise with people in this situation, but it might be more positive to review *our* 'yesterdays'—if only to work out how we got where we are, and how we too can get from yesterday to tomorrow. This is our journey.

5 When trust becomes mistrust

Numbers 14:1–12

The arrival of quails quells the unrest but the problems don't go away. There is worse to come. Step 3 is when trust becomes mistrust, beginning with Aaron (chapter 12). It's time for democracy.

Twelve men, one from each tribe, are assigned to spy out the land, and off they go. On their return, with the exception of Joshua and Caleb, who present a minority report, their overall view is that attempting entry to the land would be disastrous. The reaction of the people is violent (v. 1). The whole expedition has been a disaster. A new leader is a called for. Even Moses is feeling the heat. Whether they are simply shying at the fence or shivering on the brink, a not-uncommon response by the masses when given an opportunity to go for change, this moment calls for that delicate judgement which all leaders have to face.

In times of crisis, the cry for a strong leader to steady the nerves is understandable and makes good sense, but the issue now has moved on from food shortages to fear of what lies ahead. To counter this, the leaders need more than strength. They also need diplomacy and the capacity to deliver, and there is little evidence of either.

Churchill faced a similar situation in 1940. Food shortage was a critical problem then, but secondary to the threat of Nazism. Churchill might have got somewhere had he suggested that the German forces were 'no more than bread [meat and drink] for us' (v. 9), but had he failed, the people would have 'eaten him alive', and even after victory he was still rejected. Tough words may stir the masses (for a time), whether in office or workshop, church or club, Westminster or Washington, but if leaders are to carry their people, three things are needed.

First, they have to have the trust of all the people, not simply those immediately around them. Second, they must provide evidence for their hope, even if only a shred. Third, they must avoid all bravado and excess and not claim more than they can deliver; otherwise, they will quickly be tested and, if found wanting, just as quickly discredited.

6 A power struggle

Tensions mount as reality closes in. Cracks begin to appear, with the fearful on one hand and the potential leaders who think they can do better than the present crew on the other, giving a direct challenge to authority and leadership on two fronts.

In the first case, two Reubenites, backed by 250 'well-known men' (v. 2), confront Moses and Aaron on the grounds that they have become too big for their boots. What is in question is not their policies but their attitude. The two brothers have come from nowhere and set themselves up as leaders, and a struggling people have been happy to follow. But on the journey, attitudes have changed. People have noticed, reflected and talked, and now that things are going wrong, they feel they need to be consulted. Moses and Aaron have lost touch with their constituency, think they know best and convey the impression that they believe they are a cut above everybody else. Meanwhile, the people feel discredited and, at worst, treated like dirt. It's a typical and not unfamiliar pattern.

In the second case, the Levites (led by Korah) are claiming more territory, and Moses thinks *they* are getting too big for their boots. Already having a privileged position among the tribes, with responsibility for the tabernacle, they now want to move in on the priesthood as well.

One question we might ask is how the parties involved might have handled the conflict better. Probably, little is to be gained by digging into their situation, but, in order to glean some light from Numbers, it may be profitable to try to identify the ingredients of the struggle. This might be helpful when we find ourselves suddenly walking into a similar situation, since the ingredients repeat themselves again and again. They include murmurings and minor dissatisfactions; feelings of not being heard, being bypassed or meeting outright rejection; spotting the possibility of change and going for it. Then come confrontation, judgement, repentance and (hopefully) resolution, followed finally (but rarely) by an objective examination of what has changed. What was it worth? Who has gained and who has lost? Failure adequately to address these issues at this point may simply sow the seeds for a repeat performance.

Guidelines

- What do the 500 years of Israelite history, coming to fulfilment in 40 years of wandering in the search for the promised land, say to us about our European history and where we stand today as a community?
- Focus on one or two examples of nonconformity in your experience. To what extent do both the nonconformist and the community come up to the tests in Numbers 6?
- The Israelites might never have had the rationale for climate change that we are familiar with, but try making a list (alone or with others) of ways in which their natural readiness to cooperate with God in nature calls us to address similar situations where we could do so, but manifestly don't. Discuss your findings with your friends.
- All change involves loss as well as gain. Golden moments from yesterday, however, can provide a platform for thankfulness—whether they concern food, children growing up, churches, nations, leaders or politicians. Take a moment to think how the same changes impact differently on different groups.
- Try applying the requisites for leadership to Moses and Caleb. Then reflect on similar situations in your own experience to discover what Numbers has to offer by way of help.

16–22 October

1 Time to talk

Numbers 17:1—18:7

Life in the wilderness is tough. The mood of the community reflects the topography of the environment. They are sinking in the desert sand, the project has failed and the world is collapsing round their ears. The leaders are divided, the troops in chaos. Unable to survive where they are, it is time to move on, but somebody has to get a grip on the situation. It's time to talk—the leaders with the people, the people and the leaders with one another, and everybody with God. It is time also to count the costs.

A mutual recognition of what went wrong, and why, will be helpful, provided it can be done without harking to the past, raking over the ashes or attributing blame. Some humility and acceptance of responsibility on all sides will be a positive move. More difficult might be the rebuilding of relationships. Crises, with rebellious tribal leaders in a stand-off with Moses and Aaron (see Numbers 16), reflected increasing strife within tribes and almost certainly tensions among families and friends, winners and losers alike. Even a minor fracas can leave deep wounds that take time to heal.

Two positive steps are taken. First, to regain the confidence of the people, the leadership is clearly defined. The budding of Aaron's rod (vv. 1–11) may seem a strange way of doing this, but it worked for them. More important is the involvement of leaders from all the tribes. Leadership can never be claimed or assumed. It has to be gained and recognised. At this stage, the position of Moses seems not to be an issue, and Aaron is now established as his number two.

Second, the role of the Levites is clarified. They have always enjoyed something of a different, not to say privileged, position; but now their authority is confined to the sanctuary, as assistants to the priests, primarily responsible for the protection of the people from wrath. Nobody wants to experience the problems of the past few weeks all over again.

It's a solution, maybe, but only till next time something goes wrong. How long that might be is anybody's guess. What do you think? Hopefully, important principles have been established, from which lessons might be learned when similar situations crop up in future.

2 Time to cooperate

Numbers 20:1–13

'Next time' is not long coming. A drought hits, and here we are again. Post-crisis solutions may be short-lived, and trust in leadership can be very ephemeral.

But why, in a desert, were they so put about by a shortage of water (vv. 2, 5)? Had it never happened before? Or had they experienced drought before, found ways of dealing with it, but learned nothing from the experience about the desert's hidden water resources?

To appreciate the spiritual element of this story (as well as the practical), it helps to move beyond gasping at the miracle. How much was it a miracle, and how much a story of learning to recognise the miracle behind the miracle? God doesn't provide water out of thin air here. What he does is to work through nature to provide for his creatures. In the desert, water courses through rock formations, as a very real and natural part of his creation. Survival is about learning to cooperate with God's creation, and miracles happen when we learn to recognise that and work with it.

So why didn't these people do it? Answers can only be speculative. Possibly because they had grown up in Egypt where, although they were slaves, the provision of water and food could be taken for granted. What they learned at Meribah was that it wasn't like that everywhere. It hadn't always been like that, even in Egypt. Joseph might have been brought to Egypt in the first place through a mixture of his arrogance, his brothers' jealousy and the slickness of the slave traders, but what gave him the opportunity to get his family there as well was his perception of the way God works. Years of plenty, followed by years of famine, demonstrate how God's resources are more than adequate but always need careful husbandry. God still works like that. His world is rich in resources. There is food and energy enough for all our needs—but not if too many of us keep it for ourselves, or if we fail to husband our resources wisely.

In their 'Meribah moment', these former slaves need another Joseph. Next time, there may not be another Moses on hand to strike the rock. What we have here is a lesson in how better to cooperate with God and his creation, and the crucial importance of doing so.

3 The mouths of babes

Numbers 22:22–35

When a large group of people with a reputation for mopping up everything in their way suddenly arrive on the edge of your territory, and you know you don't have the resources to deal with them, you cry for help. So Balak, king of Moab, who doesn't want the Israelites on his doorstep, sends a messenger to Balaam, with a blank cheque, for reinforcements—though his attitude suggests that it may not be reinforcements he really wants. He would much prefer to curse the lot of them, if only he could. He also seems to work on the principle (or the assumption) that every man (or Balaam, at least) has his price.

He obviously doesn't know Balaam. Balaam can be difficult. He says, 'No'. Yahweh says, 'No'. Balaam cannot go. Under pressure, he responds more positively to a second request and agrees to go, but remains crystal clear in his own mind that he will only do what Yahweh says. Then follows a strange incident, like nothing else in Numbers—possibly a very ancient story from a pre-literal tradition, providing a mixture of irony and humour—leaving us with three things to consider.

First, in a world that thrives on all price and no principle, people, nations and businesses can all be bought until they suddenly come up against somebody who can't.

Second, is Balaam a good example of the one who can't be bought, or is he perhaps one who can but is no soft touch, and has principles for which he stands, though even he can wobble with uncertainty?

Third, who among us can help but smile at a man with a reputation as a seer who cannot see what is blindingly obvious in front of him and needs an ass to describe it to him? This is just one more example of the man of God, the insider, needing an outsider (the ass) to tell him the truth and save him from folly. Perhaps it's a hopeful sign of things to come (1 Corinthians 1:27). But full credit to Balaam, who, once the penny drops, will never surrender.

4 New community, new leader

Numbers 27:12–23

The end of a chapter. The journey over. Home at last. A new world is waiting, and a new community calls for a new leader. Choosing one's own successor is never ideal and rarely works, but there are exceptions, and theirs is a different world from ours. We can reflect on the qualities that Moses thinks are required of his successor, and the checks and balances that are necessary too. Moses identifies four qualities.

- First, Joshua has demonstrated charisma in battle. He leads from the front. He will 'lead them out and bring them in' (v. 17). First up, first back—but not until the job is done. Whether Joshua is ahead in thought as well as action is not spelt out, but is perhaps inferred.

- Second, he is close enough to Moses to continue the tradition, but with a recognition that he is not Moses and therefore cannot have the same authority.

- Third, he is someone who can maintain order and discipline, to ensure that the people 'may not be like sheep without a shepherd' (v. 17). That phrase contains an element that may not be immediately apparent to our Western ears. We think of sheep as docile, and we understand a flock without a shepherd as a congregation without a pastor, but in the Septuagint (a translation of the Old Testament from Hebrew into Greek, dating from the third century BC) 'sheep without a shepherd' often means 'a leaderless mob'. Joshua needs to be a 'toughie'.

- Fourth, he is God's man. This requires recognition by Eliezer and (independently) by the people (v. 19), with a public investiture; they have to know him and recognise his authority, and he has to know to whom he is responsible. The divine stamp is provided by the unusual method (to us) of Urim and Thummin, thought to be two single objects (despite being Hebrew plurals)—possibly sticks or pebbles, maybe one white and the other black. They functioned as sacred lots, not unlike dice. Priests appear to have used them for divination and they may have been more sophisticated and less simple than they seem. As a way of discerning the will of God, we might think them casual and unreliable, although whether they are any more so than many of our current methods is worth considering.

5 Walking in the ways of God

Numbers 33:1–10

This is the first of two important chapters in Israelite history—an end and a beginning, a looking back and a looking forward, a wandering people of God and land possession. Chapter 33 is dull and repetitive, offering little to us in terms of history, geography or spirituality, but try to enter into the experience of the Israelites and feel their emotions. For 40 years they simply 'set out… and camped', but never arrived.

Bearing in mind the people's average lifespan, 40 years was a long time. Many had been born in the wilderness; most would have seen relatives die there. Only a few would 'remember' the days in slavery, but all had lived under its shadow and would have an impression of the history—stories of the old days, long since gone and left behind; of courage and privation as they struggled day after day, hopes raised, hopes dashed, and always with a vision of a 'promised land' which never materialised. Now, today, they stand on the threshold of fulfilment.

Think of the experiences they have gone through—the high points, the low points, the fracas and the moments of cooperation; the joys and the sorrows as they married, bore children and buried their dead, all amid personal hopes and ambitions, some fulfilled, some dashed.

What does their story tell us about them as people? Something, perhaps, about their adaptability and capacity to change—40 'homes' in 40 years—or about never giving up when hope burns low; about the need for privacy and interdependence, personal rights and community needs, freedom and security, the individual and the community.

Two questions. One, as they stand on the threshold of the promised land, at the end of a struggle and the realisation of a dream, what do you sense are their predominant emotions? Thrill and satisfaction? Fear and apprehension? What do they expect to happen? Two, what do you think would happen next?

6 The land as symbol

Numbers 34:1–15

By general agreement, these verses are thought to come from a later period than other parts of the text, because there are no early records of the places mentioned. These were the boundaries of the promised land as they were in the sixth century BC. But that doesn't prevent us from entering into the emotions of a different people who had spent nearly 500 years in a totally different wilderness, culminating in the fall of Jerusalem, exile in Babylon and a return, ready to establish a new nation. They too needed roots, a past and (perhaps most of all) their own territory. What aspects of the past did they value and what did they wish to preserve?

Certainly not the slavery (there is no suggestion whatsoever of going back to 'the good old days of Egypt'), but a recognition of and a certain pride in their story—from humble beginnings with Abraham, to Joseph, who saved the mighty Egypt from a dire famine; then years of immigrant growth and service in a land which was not theirs. A few hundred years later, Moses, a charismatic leader, led them from slavery to freedom, though not without a struggle and much deprivation. In the course of all that, they found a faith, embraced a God who first embraced them, and constructed a community with meaning, purpose and a set of values, embodied in a religious structure. That was something of value and, as each generation gave way to the next, they intended to cling on to it. The land was, and still is, crucial to complete the jigsaw. Today they stand on the brink, about to claim it for Yahweh and themselves.

Some people and some nations will read this and want to say, 'This is our story' as they recognise and acknowledge it with some pride and satisfaction as part of their similar heritage.

Numbers is an encouragement to acknowledge our past, to appreciate the moment when we stand on the brink of change (any change) and recognise all the emotions that go with it, to know not only when to move and when to stick but also what to embrace and what to leave behind. Numbers is our story and, at many points, is personal, national and ecclesiastical.

Guidelines

- Use your own experience to imagine the conversations between the people in general, between those closest to the leaders, and especially between priests and Levites when they met socially, once the leadership question was sorted. What would today's media have made of it?

- Identify a 'Meribah moment' in your own experience or that of your friends, family or community. Work out in practical terms what it might call for and how you could play your part in it.

- On a scale of one to ten, where would you place yourself compared with Balaam, if one is 'nothing like' and ten is 'identical'.

- How do Moses' requirements for leadership compare with the qualities we look for when we appoint leaders? Can you imagine how the way we choose our leaders must appear to someone brought up in a totally different culture?

- When John Steinbeck's 'Oakies' entered California, they found not only that it was not all they had hoped for but also that they had lost the thrill and purpose of the journey: they had nowhere else to go. Possession of the land has to be a means, not an end. What is needed to keep alive the vision when life becomes more ordinary and routine?

- One scholar has suggested that, on entering the promised land, the Israelites may have discovered that 'a future becoming' by the continued 'walking in the ways of God' is more important than any arrival. Starting from there, how different might our life be if we were to focus on 'becoming' rather than 'arriving'?

FURTHER READING

Bruce M. Metzger and Michael D. Coogan (eds), *The Oxford Companion to the Bible*, Oxford University Press, 1993.

John W. Rogerson and Judith M. Lieu (eds), *The Oxford Handbook of Biblical Studies*, Oxford University Press, 2006.

John Barton and John Muddiman (eds), *Cambridge Companion to Biblical Interpretation*, Cambridge University Press, 1998.

Charles M. Laymon (ed.), *Interpreter's One-Volume Commentary on the Bible*, Abingdon Press, 1971.

Matthew Black and H.H. Rowley, *Peake's Commentary on the Bible*, Nelson, 1962.

Justification by faith

Over the next two weeks, we are going to think about the biblical doctrine of justification by faith. Although this important subject is always worthy of attention, now is a particularly appropriate time to consider it, as this year is the 500th anniversary of an event that changed the face of Christian history. On 31 October 1517, a young lecturer in theology at the University of Wittenberg, named Martin Luther, posted 95 'theses' on the door of All Saints' Church (often known as the Castle Church).

Although this may seem a strange and dramatic action to us, in fact it seems to have been a recognised way of raising an issue for consideration. The topic that Martin Luther raised in his theses was that of 'indulgences'. Indulgences were certificates issued by the Roman Catholic Church which declared that a person might face less time of purification in purgatory in return for the payment of a fee. At this point in his career, Martin Luther's main concern was not the doctrine of justification by faith. Most scholars agree that he did not come to a settled theological understanding of justification until some time later. Yet this doctrine soon became of central importance to Luther.

In these notes, we will read some texts which were significant in Luther's thinking and are central to the doctrine of justification by faith. In each case, we will hear a little of Luther's voice but we will also attempt to read the text in the light of further scholarship from beyond Luther's day. During the first week, we will focus on some Old Testament passages before turning to the New Testament during the second week.

Quotations are taken from the New Revised Standard Version of the Bible.

23–29 October

1 Trust reckoned as righteousness

Genesis 15

The doctrine of justification by faith is not a Pauline doctrine; it is a biblical doctrine. Numerous Old Testament texts contribute ideas that were later brought together in the fully formed doctrine.

 23–29 October

It all starts with God's promise. Genesis 15 recounts Abram's dramatic encounter with Yahweh (the covenant name of God). Here, Yahweh reaffirms his covenant promise to Abram. In particular, he confirms that, despite all the circumstances, Abram will have a son and heir (vv. 2–4). Verse 6 then affirms that Abram 'believed the Lord, and the Lord reckoned it to him as righteousness'. Similar language is found in Psalm 106:30–31 with reference to the action of Phineas (see Numbers 25). Abram's attitude of trust in God, affirmed in Genesis 15:6, later becomes significant in the writings of Paul (see Romans 4:3, 5; Galatians 3:6). Luther commented on these words:

Nor does God require anything greater of man than that he attribute to Him His glory and His divinity; that is, that he regard Him, not as an idol but as God, who has regard for him, listens to him, shows mercy to him, helps him, etc… Therefore faith justifies because it renders to God what is due Him; whoever does this is righteous.

Luther's Works, 26: Lectures on Galatians 1535 (Concordia, 1963), p. 227

We will look at the references to this passage in Paul's letters later, but for now we note several points in the text of Genesis 15. First, Yahweh reveals himself to Abram and declares that he himself is Abram's 'very great reward' (v. 1, NIV). At the heart of God's dealing with humanity is not the various benefits that he may bring, but a relationship with God himself that he has established. Second, Yahweh reiterates the promise given in Genesis 12:1–2. He once again promises to provide Abram with both descendants (v. 5) and a land (v. 7). Third, Yahweh reminds Abram of his prior act of grace (v. 7) and presents that as the foundation for Abram to have confidence that God will fulfil his promises. Fourth, Yahweh commits himself to faithfulness by means of a solemn ceremony (vv. 17–18). At the heart of the doctrine of justification lie God's gracious promise and the call to trust him. This is as true for us today as it was for Abram.

2 Hidden sins

Psalm 32

Justification has to do with declaring a person to be just, to be in the right. Yet the various books of the Bible are consistent in declaring that all humanity is in a state of rebellion against God and no one is righteous (Psalm 14:1–3; see also the collection of texts cited by Paul in Romans 3:10–18).

Many people would doubtless find this perspective on humanity very pessi-mistic and perhaps even offensive. Some would object that they are decent citizens and, while they might accept that 'nobody's perfect', they would claim that they are 'doing their best'. But Psalm 32 offers an alternative basis for confidence. It declares that the 'happy' one is not the person who has committed no sin (for such a person does not exist) but the one 'whose transgression is forgiven, whose sin is covered' (v. 1).

The Psalms were very important in shaping the thought of Martin Luther with respect to justification. Luther comments on these words:

Righteous people, however, do not hide their iniquity, do not become angry, do not grow impatient even when they are wronged; for they do not feel that they can be wronged, since they find no righteousness in themselves. These are the blessed to whom God remits iniquity and cancels it because they confess it. Since they do not hide and cover their sin, God covers and hides it.

Luther's Works, 14: Selected Psalms III (Concordia, 1958), p. 150

In this Psalm, we note that the language of 'counting' is used once again. The Hebrew verb *chashav* is used in both Genesis 15:6 and Psalm 32:2. This term, in the wider context of the psalm, suggests that Yahweh is not unaware of a person's sin and rebellion. In fact, while that sin is kept to oneself, it causes great distress (vv. 3–4). But when it is confessed, God for-gives it (v. 5). So the psalmist presents God not as a fearful opponent from whom one must hide, but as a refuge to whom one should run (vv. 6–7). The distinction between the righteous and the wicked is not whether they have committed sin (they all have) but whether they trust God and have their sins hidden by him (vv. 8–11).

3: The sacrifice of a broken heart

Psalm 51

King David is a remarkable figure. Samuel calls him 'a man after [God's] own heart' (1 Samuel 13:14), and God promises that one of his line will rule over an eternal kingdom (2 Samuel 7:12–16). Yet he is guilty of horrendous wickedness against Bathsheba and Uriah (2 Samuel 11—12). According to the title of the psalm, David wrote it when confronted with his sin.

The fundamental theme of the psalm is stated in the balanced plea of verse 1. A repeated request ('have mercy' / 'blot out my transgressions') relates to the repeated acknowledgement of the foundation for that request ('your steadfast love' / 'your abundant mercy'). The character of God is the basis of the psalmist's hope. Verse 2 also emphasises his need for cleansing.

The psalmist acknowledges two things—his own sin and the justice of God (vv. 3–5). Surprisingly, he considers himself accountable primarily to God rather than to the humans he has wronged. His sin brings down the just judgement of God. Internal transformation, not simply external correction, is now required (vv. 6–12), and only God can accomplish this. Only God can create a clean heart and renew a right spirit (v. 10).

Later, the psalmist declares that a 'broken and contrite heart' is more acceptable to God than burnt offerings and sacrifices (vv. 16–17). How astonishing! The Torah is full of regulations relating to the sacrificial system, yet a burnt offering will not restore fellowship with God. God seeks a heart that is turned from sin and towards him.

Luther comments on the psalmist's vision of God's character:

Now look how beautifully David combines these two things: first, that God is merciful, that is, that He freely blesses us undeserving ones; second, that he gives us the forgiveness of sins, which we accept by faith through the Holy Spirit and His promises. If God did not freely forgive, we should have no satisfaction and no remedy left.

Luther's Works, 12: Selected Psalms I (Concordia, 1955), p. 324

God's merciful and gracious character, and his act of new creation, are the psalmist's only hope, and the same is true for us.

4 Forgiveness and freedom

Psalm 130

This psalm is one of the 'Songs of Ascents' (Psalms 120—134). It has been described as a 'penitential psalm', expressing deep repentance. According to James Mays, 'Luther called it "a proper master and doctor of Scripture", by which he meant that the psalm teaches the basic truth of the gospel' (*Psalms*, Westminster John Knox, 1994, p. 405).

The psalm begins with a plaintive cry to the Lord from 'the depths' (v. 1). The precise nature of these depths is not explicitly stated, but the emphasis on faults and forgiveness in the remainder of the psalm suggests that a sense of personal guilt before God is the primary issue.

Despite the mournful tone of the opening words, the psalm quickly moves into expressions of hope and confidence in the Lord.

Verses 3–4 are particularly important, where the psalmist acknowledges that if God chose to keep a record of sin, then nobody would have reason for hope. He is confident, however, that this is not, in fact, the attitude of God, and his confidence lies in the revealed character of the Lord. Luther says:

If anyone does not fear God, he does not implore, nor is he forgiven. In order, therefore, to gain God's grace, He and He alone is to be feared, just as He alone forgives.

Luther's Works, 14: Selected Psalms III (Concordia, 1958), p. 191

Luther is certainly correct that the psalmist connects a reverence for God (a healthy 'fear') with forgiveness. I wonder, however, if Luther has reversed the logical order of these things. It seems to me that the astonishing news that the holy God of Israel should pardon sin is the basis of the reverence that is rightly to be shown for the Lord. The better our understanding of the remarkable combination of justice and mercy in God's character, the more appropriately we will approach him.

This is not simply a matter of personal confidence. It is to be the confidence of Israel. The final verses of the psalm encourage Israel to hope in the Lord, who demonstrates covenant love and loyalty and who is able to redeem. The repeated reference to redemption in verses 7 and 8 indicates God's power to release individuals and whole peoples from the power of sin that ensnares them. He does this still.

5 Righteousness and salvation

Isaiah 51:1–16

In the early verses of chapter 51 of the prophecy of Isaiah, the prophet presents a beautiful poetic description of the relationship between 'righteousness' and 'salvation'. Three times, these two terms stand together in Hebrew parallelism (vv. 5, 6, 8):

I will bring near my deliverance swiftly,
my salvation has gone out…

but my salvation will be for ever,
and my deliverance will never be ended…

but my deliverance will be for ever,
and my salvation to all generations.

Although the NRSV disguises the language somewhat by sometimes using the word 'righteousness' (as in verse 1: 'Listen to me, you that pursue righteousness…' and verse 7: 'Listen to me, you who know righteousness'), and sometimes the word 'deliverance' (as in the verses quoted above), it is the Hebrew root *ts-d-q* that is used throughout.

God's 'righteousness' is his character. God's 'salvation' is what he accomplishes on account of that character. Speaking of this salvation, Luther comments on verse 8:

Because the Word will stand forever, its victory is forever.

Luther's Works, 17: Lectures on Isaiah Chapters 40—66 (Concordia, 1972), p. 200

If we are tempted to regard God's 'righteousness' as a rather cold, sterile idea, we should allow the rich hopefulness of this passage to shape our understanding in a fresh way.

These prophetic words are addressed to a people who will experience exile and captivity, but the hope remains that God's righteous character will lead to salvation. The concept of God's unending, glorious salvation is developed further in the New Testament, going beyond the restoration of Zion (Isaiah 51:3) to restoration and renewal of the heavens and the earth (Revelation 21:1–8). Both Isaiah 51 and Revelation 21 express the two-edged reality of God's righteousness: those who acknowledge him will know the wonder of his salvation, whereas those who stand against him will know his righteous judgement.

6 Faith in the faithful God

Habakkuk 1:1—2:4

The prophecy of Habakkuk is classed in English Bibles as one of the 'minor prophets' (minor in length, not importance) at the end of the Old Testament. Many Bible readers have difficulty locating it! Yet Habakkuk 2:4b is cited twice by Paul and once by the author of Hebrews (Romans 1:17; Galatians 3:11; Hebrews 10:38). For Paul, these words encapsulate the gospel.

The prophecy, dating probably from the last few years of the seventh century BC, is a series of statements by Habakkuk followed by responses from Yahweh. It opens with a lament from the prophet: 'O Lord, how long shall I cry for help, and you will not listen?' (1:2). As he observes life in Judah, he sees that the Torah is powerless to stop injustice (v. 4). What is Yahweh going to do? Yahweh's response is unexpected and shocking: he will bring judgement on Judah by a godless power, the Babylonians (vv. 5–11). In response to this shocking revelation, Habakkuk holds on to Yahweh's justice (v. 12). Yet he also struggles with apparent injustice, challenging the Lord's seeming tolerance of evil (v. 13).

In spite of his confusion, Habakkuk determines that he will patiently wait to see the outcome (2:1). Yahweh then counsels patience and trust. God's justice may not be apparent, but he will be true to his word (v. 3). Verse 4 contrasts two ways of living. First, there is the proud person, whose spirit is not just, and then there is 'the righteous'. The Hebrew description of this person might be translated in either of two ways: 'the righteous will live by his faith' or 'the righteous will live by his/its faithfulness'. The Greek translation of the verse adds a further option: 'the righteous one will live by my faith/faithfulness'.

Luther read these words (as used in Galatians) as a reference to faith in Christ:

We want to retain and extol this faith which God has called faith, that is, a true and certain faith that has no doubts about God or the divine promises or the forgiveness of sins through Christ.

Luther's Works, 26: Lectures on Galatians 1535, p. 270

The believer must trust in God who is righteous, even when injustice seems to prevail. But that trust depends on the faithfulness, the absolute trustworthiness, of God.

Guidelines

We have looked at a selection of Old Testament passages relating to justification, drawing on narrative, poetry and prophecy. These individual passages must be read in the context of the overall narrative of the Old Testament. They assume certain fundamental elements of the biblical worldview: an original pristine world created by the eternal God who declares all he has made to be 'very good' (Genesis 1); a righteous standard established by this good and just God in the context of a relationship of grace and closeness (Genesis 2); and an act of wilful disobedience on the part of humanity that ruptures the relationship between God and humanity (Genesis 3). Consider the following themes and the suggested responses.

- God initiates a restored relationship. The narrative of Genesis 15 indicates that God takes on himself the ultimate responsibility for the solemn covenant commitment. *Response:* Reflect on God's commitment to bring us back into relationship with him through Christ.
- God remains a righteous judge, even as he shows mercy. His mercy is not an indication that he treats injustice or wrongdoing lightly. *Response:* Consider how God's ultimate justice is comforting in this unjust world.
- God provided the sacrificial system as a means of demonstrating the seriousness of sin and pointing to the means by which sin would ultimately be dealt with. Yet he is more interested in the attitude of a person's heart than in the actions they perform. *Response:* Pray that God would give you a heart that turns humbly to him.
- Although there is no escaping humanity's culpability before God, God repeatedly indicates that his desire is to show forgiveness. *Response:* Thank God for his willingness to forgive.
- There is a close relationship between God's 'righteousness' and his 'salvation'. God's righteous character leads to action that brings rescue to those who are in a hopeless situation. *Response:* Praise God for salvation in his Messiah, Jesus.
- Even when circumstances are perplexing, God remains righteous and worthy of our trust. *Response:* Pray for confidence in God's character during difficult days.

1 God's righteousness revealed

Romans 1:1–17

Paul writes to the Christians in Rome in order to explain his gospel to them, a gospel that is 'the power of God that brings salvation to everyone who believes' (1:16, NIV). Paul then explains the reason for his confidence in the gospel, drawing on the words of Habakkuk 2:4.

'Righteousness' is a key term in Romans. It can have various connotations, depending on the context. It can refer to an aspect of the character of God: God is righteous. He is always upright and acts justly. 'Righteousness' has also been understood, notably by Martin Luther, as 'saving righteousness'. Luther once regarded the idea of 'the righteousness of God' as oppressive, as he explains in the Preface to the Complete Edition of his Latin Works (1545). Luther once felt that this righteous God stood against him. Nothing Luther could do would placate God. Then a change occurred, as Luther considered the text of Romans 1:17. He began to understand 'the righteousness of God' as God's gracious gift, received by faith. The impact of this new understanding was that Luther felt liberated, as if he had been reborn and had entered paradise.

We will look at the 'righteousness of God' in detail in the coming days. For now, we recognise the remarkable impact of this text on a man who was weighed down by sin and was then set free.

We may also note, in passing, Paul's comment that this righteousness is 'revealed' (v. 17, *apokaluptetai*). The Greek term gives us the English word 'apocalyptic'. Scholars such as J. Louis Martyn and Douglas Campbell use this term to describe an interpretation of Paul in which God breaks into human experience in a way that is dramatically different from any previous revelation. Paul's language of 'revelation' in Romans and Galatians does provide some foundation for describing his theology as 'apocalyptic', but this does not require acceptance of the interpretation of Martyn, Campbell and others. Paul's frequent reference to Old Testament texts and narratives suggests that he regards the events of Christ's life as the culmination of a single long story.

2   Justified by faith in Christ

Galatians 2:15–21

Paul's letter to the Galatians is a passionate yet careful plea to the Christians in Galatia to hold fast to the true gospel. Paul explained earlier how God called him to declare the good news. In the verses we are reading, he moves into theological argument. The key terms in this passage have been debated in recent academic literature, but we will consider the discussion only briefly.

Paul indicates common agreement that no human can be 'justified' by 'works of the law'. The terms 'justification' and 'righteousness' are quite different in English, but the Greek words have the same root. Most scholars agree that the language relates to the law court. The terms may describe either the character of the judge or the declaration made regarding those who stand before the judge.

The term 'works of the law' has often been interpreted as a reference to 'legalism'—the attempt to earn favour before God. This interpretation was challenged by a number of scholars, notably E.P. Sanders, who argued that the Jewish view is better described as 'covenantal nomism'. The discussion developed further when the Dead Sea Scrolls were discovered (from 1947) and a document named 4QMMT was discovered. The initials 'MMT', used to designate this document found in cave 4 at Qumran (4Q), come from a Hebrew phrase in the text meaning 'some of the works of the law'. James Dunn, a proponent of the so-called 'new perspective on Paul', suggested that this phrase might relate to so-called Jewish 'boundary markers' (such as circumcision, sabbath and food laws). Dunn would now acknowledge that it has a broader meaning. Perhaps the best way to understand the phrase is as 'what the law requires'. In any case, Paul is clear that nobody can be right with God on the basis of their actions.

Instead, they must exercise 'faith' or 'trust'. In Galatians 2:20, Paul shows that his new status is not simply a 'legal fiction' but a new life united to Christ by faith. Luther explains further:

Faith takes hold of Christ and has Him present, enclosing Him as the ring encloses the gem. And whoever is found having this faith in the Christ who is grasped in the heart, him God accounts as righteous.

Luther's Works, 26: Lectures on Galatians 1535, p. 132

God's just declaration should be understood in the context of union with the Son of God by faith, based on his love-motivated sacrifice.

3 The God who is just and justifies

Romans 3:1–31

Paul, in Romans 3:21–26, declares that God is able to 'justify' those who are guilty, and yet to demonstrate his justice. Part of Paul's intention in Romans is to argue that God is not unjust (see Romans 3:5).

Paul establishes that no human being is 'righteous' (3:10–20), but, if no human being is righteous, how can a righteous judge declare anyone righteous? Would this not compromise the judge (see Isaiah 5:20)? There is no doubt about the guilt of those who stand accused, and the sentence is death (Romans 6:23). Yet, in the gospel, God has made known a righteousness that brings life to those who have faith in Jesus the Messiah. So how can God be just if he 'justifies' (declares righteous) those who are plainly not righteous?

Paul explains that Jesus Christ has accomplished 'redemption' (a word for 'freedom' that has echoes of the release of the enslaved Israelites from Egypt). Redemption was achieved as God presented Jesus as a 'sacrifice of atonement'. This phrase translates the Greek term *hilasterion*, sometimes translated as 'means of expiation' or 'propitiation'. Each of these translations has some merit. 'Expiation' has to do with the removal of sin. 'Propitiation' has to do with turning away God's righteous anger. The question of translation was the subject of a dispute between C.H. Dodd and Leon Morris. In my view, Morris was correct: God's righteous anger is a biblical concept. But Jesus' death (indicated by the word 'blood') involved both the cleansing of sin and the averting of judgement, so there is no conflict between the two words.

Then Paul explains why God did this: 'to demonstrate his righteousness' (or 'justice') (v. 25, NIV). First, God demonstrates that he does not overlook sin. Paul explains that no animal sacrifice ever truly dealt with sin; however, God did not hold humans accountable for those sins at the time but 'passed over' them for a time (v. 25). Then, in Christ, these sins were dealt with completely. Luther explains:

For the sins of all, both those who have gone before as well as those who will follow, are forgiven through Christ alone.

Luther's Works, 25: Lectures on Romans (Concordia, 1972), p. 249

In this way, God is both just and the one who justifies sinners. That is truly good news.

4 Abraham's faith

Galatians 3:1–14

Paul's letter to the Galatians quickly becomes a dense argument. The argument continues in chapter 3 with a combination of passionate rebuke, powerful rhetoric and rich theological reflection. In these verses, Paul first asks a series of rhetorical questions that focus on the experience of the Galatians when they first became Christians and received the Spirit of God. How, he asks, did that experience come about? By faith? Or by some human achievement? The answer, apparently, should be obvious to them. It was by faith.

Paul's focus on faith leads him to the foundational story of Abraham and particularly to the reference to Abraham's faith in Genesis 15:6. This citation leads him on to argue that those who respond to God's promise in faith are marked as Abraham's children by that very faith, and that they share in the blessing he received.

Those who rely on 'the works of the law' (discussed earlier), on the other hand, are under a curse (in contrast to the blessing mentioned in verse 9). In verse 12, Paul again draws on the Old Testament, this time Leviticus 18:5. This verse suggests that if anyone does not fully conform with the requirements of the law, the curse will fall on that person. That is clearly bad news, because no human being does live perfectly. But Paul than draws on Deuteronomy 21:23 to argue that Christ has borne the curse for his people (v. 13). So, despite the reality of sin in the Christian's life, which deserves God's curse, those who believe in Jesus experience the blessing of Abraham, in accordance with God's promise to bless the nations, because Jesus has borne the curse in their place.

In a version of one of his most famous sayings, Luther comments on the citation of Genesis 15:

Thus a Christian man is righteous and a sinner at the same time, holy and profane, an enemy of God and a child of God.

Luther's Works, 26: Lectures on Galatians 1535, p. 232

Not only may Christians experience comfort, knowing that they experience the blessing promised to Abraham because of what Jesus has done, but also they should be motivated to mission, knowing that they have been blessed in order to bring blessing to the nations.

5 The righteousness from God

Philippians 3

Following a generally positive section of Philippians, in which Paul speaks warmly of the examples of humility seen in Jesus Christ and also in his colleagues Timothy and Epaphroditus, chapter 3 takes a darker turn. It is clear that Paul is concerned for the welfare of the Philippians in a way that is similar (though not identical) to his concern for the Galatian Christians. In the early section of this chapter, Paul not only warns the Philippians in very strong terms against those who put confidence in the physical sign of circumcision and demand that others do so too; he also speaks of his own experience. He provides some autobiographical details, in a similar way to Galatians 1. These details shed considerable light on Paul's pre-Christian life. He had a privileged life in many ways, but it has been relativised by Christ.

Paul's comments on righteousness here are important (although Luther mentions them only in passing). In verse 9 he contrasts two kinds of righteousness: 'not having a righteousness of my own that comes from the law, but one that comes through faith in Christ, the righteousness from God based on faith'. The balance of this statement is striking. In fact, the phrase translated 'righteousness from God' by the NRSV might also be translated 'righteousness of God'. In his recent major commentary on Romans (Eerdmans, 2016), Richard Longenecker distinguishes two senses of 'righteousness': the 'attributive' sense, meaning the righteous character of God and of his actions; and the 'communicative' sense, meaning a gift that God gives to his people. Some scholars have resisted the idea of a 'communicative' sense of the word. Longenecker, however, is persuaded that both senses of the word are present in Paul's writings and he believes that Philippians 3:9 is a particularly clear example of the communicative sense. Paul is not discussing the character of God here. Rather, he speaks of his own status, which comes either by his own privileges and efforts or by trusting entirely in Christ.

Paul rejoices that his righteousness does not depend on his background or accomplishments, but on what Christ has achieved on his behalf. It comes as a gift from God. As Christians, we are to place our reliance in the same place.

6 Raised to life for our justification

Romans 4 illustrates the profound importance of the narrative of the Old Testament in the thought of the apostle Paul. Here, Paul reflects on the experience of Abraham, recognised as father of the people of Israel. He pays particular attention to the words of Genesis 15:6 ('Abraham believed God, and it was reckoned to him as righteousness'). Paul argues that this event took place before Abraham was circumcised, and that Abraham's standing before God depended, therefore, not on his act of obedience but on his trust in God's promise.

At the end of this chapter, Paul uses a striking expression. Christ, says Paul, 'was handed over to death for our trespasses and was raised for our justification' (v. 25). In this balanced statement, which some have regarded as an early creedal or confessional statement, Paul highlights the significance of two key moments in the experience of Jesus: his death and his resurrection. The belief that Christ died 'for our trespasses' is relatively familiar (see also 1 Corinthians 15:3), but the idea that he was 'raised for our justification' is less familiar. Yet this fits well with Paul's view, expressed elsewhere, that both Jesus' death and his resurrection—not solely his death—were essential elements in God's act of salvation.

Luther recognised this dynamic. He writes:

The death of Christ is the death of sin, and His resurrection is the life of righteousness, because through His death He has made satisfaction for sin, and through His resurrection He has brought us righteousness.

Luther's Works, 25: Lectures on Romans, p. 284

The resurrection of Jesus is a crucial element of the Christian gospel. It declares God's seal of approval on all that Jesus accomplished in his life and death. It shows that when Jesus presented himself as a sacrifice—acting as both high priest and sacrificial offering—his offering was, like Abel's in Genesis 4, accepted.

We may look to the historical event of the resurrection and be confident that Jesus was raised for our justification.

Guidelines

Much of what was said in last week's 'Guidelines' remains applicable as we look back on the various New Testament texts we have read. You may find it helpful to read over those comments again. Consider also these themes and the suggested responses.

- God *reveals* his righteousness; it is not a human discovery. 'Righteousness' may refer to either the righteous character of God or the status he confers on sinners. As Luther knew all too well, it is not good news for unquestionably guilty sinners to discover that there is a perfectly righteous judge. Where righteousness is mentioned in connection with the gospel, we should consider that it may have the communicative sense of a gift. *Response:* Give thanks for the supremely good news that the righteous God has revealed himself to sinful humans like us.

- The gospel is that justification comes freely as a gift, received by means of faith in Jesus Christ. All that the Old Testament sacrificial system pointed to is brought to completion in Christ. If we are to understand our status before God correctly, we must understand that we have hope only as we are united to Christ by faith. *Response:* Pray for faith in Christ, in spite of your doubts.

- It is not good news that sins are forgiven if, thereby, the righteousness of God (in the attributive sense, describing his character) is compromised. Therefore, it is truly good news that God has acted in Christ's life, death and resurrection in such a way that he is both just and the one who justifies the unrighteous. *Response:* Give thanks for the unchanging righteous character of God.

- Justification is not simply a matter of looking backwards to God dealing with sin on the cross. The resurrection indicates that God's people are justified in order that they might enter fully into the resurrection life that God has purposed for his people. *Response:* Take a few moments to consider the fullness of resurrection life that is at the heart of Christian hope.

- Although there has been much debate over key biblical passages since Martin Luther's day, and although some of Luther's judgements have been overtaken by recent research, we may give thanks to God for the life and work of Martin Luther, who emphasised justification by faith in a way that it surely deserved. *Response:* Give thanks that God worked through Martin Luther in his service and that he still works through his people today.

FURTHER READING

Martin Luther, *Luther's Works*, Concordia/Fortress, various dates.

Alister E. McGrath, *Iustitia Dei: A history of the Christian doctrine of justification*, Cambridge University Press (3rd edn), 2005.

Thomas R. Schreiner, *Faith Alone: The doctrine of justification*, Zondervan, 2015.

Brian Vickers, *Justification by Grace through Faith*, Presbyterian and Reformed, 2015.

Stephen Westerholm, *Justification Reconsidered: Rethinking a Pauline theme*, Eerdmans, 2013.

Tom Wright, *Justification: God's plan and Paul's vision*, SPCK, 2009.

Luther on the Psalms

Luther's *Summaries of the Psalms* was published in 1532, as a companion to reading, singing and praying the Psalter. Luther was clear that there was little he could add to what the Psalms accomplished when they were prayed through, sung and read. Luther believed in the 'natural sense of scriptures'— that they could be read and understood naturally, without aid or explanation. So he set himself the task of writing a commentary that was deliberately minimalist, to prevent his own text from coming between the person encountering the Psalms and the voice of God speaking through these scriptures.

Luther's devotional approach to the Psalms was twofold. First, he divided them into five types: gratitude, comfort, prayer, instruction and prophecy. He acknowledged that many of the Psalms were combinations of these types: gratitude, prayer and comfort, for example, characterise Psalm 23. Second, and more unusually, he held that each psalm flowed out of one of the ten commandments and also out of the petitions in the Lord's Prayer. In practice, in terms of the ten commandments, Luther drew mainly on the first three—worshipping one God, honouring God, and hearing and obeying the commands of God's word.

Our pattern for the next fortnight will be to use Luther's fivefold typology of the Psalms—gratitude, comfort, prayer, instruction and prophecy—beginning and ending each week with psalms of gratitude or thanks, thereby acknowledging God's faithfulness at the end of a week (Saturday), in preparation for worship on Sunday, and at the start of a new working week (Monday). Occasionally, and where appropriate, we will also follow Luther's explicitly devotional approach, drawing in the Lord's Prayer and the ten commandments.

Above all else, these notes seek only to accompany you in prayerful reading—not to get in the way, to come between you and the text or to eclipse what God may be saying to you afresh through his word. So read the psalm first, reflectively, slowly and deliberatively, praying with your mind, heart and breath as the words are taken in. (I recommend reading Martin Laird, *Into the Silent Land: The practice of contemplation*, DLT, 2006, to aid your contemplation and prayer.) As you read these psalms, may God feed you in soul and body, nourish your mind and touch your heart.

Quotations are taken from the New Revised Standard Version of the Bible.

1 Gratitude: God's grace is boundless

Psalm 103

Luther's approach to the Psalms was primarily devotional. Like a chef preparing simple, exquisite ingredients, he thought he needed to do very little with this most beautiful soul-food. Like a craftsman given a beautiful, striking painting to frame, he sought only to find the most handsome, complementary surround—never taking the eye of the beholder away from the picture. So Luther said, 'I prefer to see the text stand alone by itself, unmixed with anything else. Some of these summaries are really brief commentary… With this, may God bless you. Amen.'

His claim that the Psalms also flowed out of, or belonged to, phrases in the Lord's Prayer should be understood in the context of one of his major convictions—that the Psalms testify to Christ, even though (of course) he is never explicitly mentioned. Luther believed that the psalmist's celebration of God's love, forgiveness, grace and blessing pointed to a fulfilment in Christ. And so he advocated a prayerful, disciplined and holy engagement with the Psalms, so that we may encounter the grace and forgiveness that God reveals through them.

So what does Psalm 103 tell us? It says that, to God, we are never forgotten. Nothing can separate us from God's steadfast, everlasting love and faithfulness to us. God assures us of this, and Christ embodies it in his life, death and resurrection. As Luther says of this psalm, 'What we need and what saves us all comes to pass in Christ.' God does not deal with us according to our sins but according to his abounding grace. Our response to God's free and unmerited grace is this: to keep our covenant with God and to remember to do his commandments (v. 18), always remembering that we are not rewarded according to our sins. Rather, we have grace, blessing and forgiveness lavished upon us. God abounds in steadfast love (vv. 4, 8, 10).

The psalmist gives thanks that God is compassionate and gracious, 'even though' (as Luther says in his commentary) 'we are frail and unsteady creatures'. 'Our days are but as grass,' says the psalmist, 'and like a flower of the field' (v. 15); we are here today and gone tomorrow. But the steadfast love of the Lord is everlasting. Our lives may be short but they are rooted in God's time and grounded in his eternal love for us.

2 Comfort: God comforts us in distress

C.S. Lewis once remarked that God whispers in our pleasure, but shouts in our pain. He meant that God is not deaf to our suffering and that God is sometimes loudest when we are at our least receptive. Luther says of Psalm 77 that God is 'there to help us when we think that we are totally abandoned… God never abandons when things go ill.'

Psalm 77 is a psalm of instruction, but specifically about comfort. God's gift of comfort is to those in the deepest, darkest abyss. When we feel most abandoned, God is closer than ever. A salutary story is told of Geoffrey Studdert Kennedy (or Woodbine Willie, as he was called), a much-loved army chaplain in World War I.

In the trenches one day, Studdert Kennedy heard of a small party of soldiers marooned in no man's land, trying to save a comrade. They had gone out to comfort him because they could not bear to hear his cries of pain and suffering, but now they were caught under fire, unable to move. With their comrade, they were crying out in distress, in the darkness of the mud and mayhem of war. Studdert Kennedy felt he had to be with them, to comfort them, so he crawled out, under fire, to meet them. 'Who are you?' asked one startled soldier when Studdert Kennedy eventually reached them. 'The Church,' he replied. 'What on earth are you doing *here*?' asked the soldier. 'My job,' replied Studdert Kennedy.

As Luther knew, the Psalms can point us forward to the life and work of Jesus—and Jesus, of course, knew abandonment and desolation. The Gospels tell us that we find Jesus, and therefore true ministry, in tough, tiring and trying places—not necessarily at the place where we are at our freshest or best or our most confident.

Dennis Potter, the playwright, had something wise to say about comfort, but it may be difficult to receive: 'Religion is not always the bandage—sometimes it is the wound.' Yes, we turn to Christ and the church for comfort, hope and healing. But in receiving them, we are marked by the cross, which requires us to expend our own lives sacrificially in offering and gift. Studdert Kennedy understood that the God who brings us comfort sometimes also uses us to bring it to others.

3 Prayer: pleading in prayer

Psalm 102

According to the American writer Anne Lamott, the prayers of the Daily Offices can be simply summarised. Morning Prayer, she suggests, can be condensed into a single word: 'Whatever'. And Evening Prayer needs only two words: 'Ah, well'. Lamott says elsewhere that there are only three other prayers, really: 'Help', 'Thanks' and 'Wow!' We perhaps spend too much time pleading, not enough time thanking, and very little time just saying of and to God, 'Wow'. Lamott would also agree with Woody Allen: 'If you want to make God laugh, tell him about your plans.'

Some of the great prayers in the English language are actually *about* prayer. They teach us to pray, as Jesus did. We might think of Cranmer's majestic Collect for Purity: 'Almighty God, unto whom all hearts are open, all desires known, and from whom no secrets are hidden, cleanse the thoughts of our hearts.' In other words, sift and sanctify our desires and dreams. Do not give us what we want, but do give us what we need, and what is good for us. As Luther says of Psalm 102, 'The fathers of old… yearn and call for the kingdom of grace promised in Christ.'

Jesus, in teaching his disciples to pray, keeps the matter simple. God will answer your prayers. He listens to persistence. But sometimes the answer is 'No'. We are to hallow the name of God, seek the coming of his kingdom and name our needs—*not* our desires. God can always see what we want: 'no secrets are hidden,' as Cranmer says. We are to ask forgiveness for our wrongdoing, forgive others and pray for deliverance. The psalmist knows that God will not hide his face from us. When we call, God listens.

Where does this lead us? God can only give good things. He can only bless; he does not curse. But we need wisdom to see what he is giving as he blesses us. Prayer, then, is attuning the soul to God's heart and mind, our wisdom being something of an echo of the wisdom that comes from above.

Mature prayer is not a shopping list to place before God. It is the self placed before God, so that the needs and desires of the world and the individual may be set before the true light that cleanses 'the thoughts of our hearts', enabling us to love and worship more perfectly.

4 Instruction: who will dwell on God's holy hill?

Psalm 15

I have dwelt on the holy hill. The little village of Cuddesdon, Oxfordshire, where I lived and worked for ten years, has a theological college (founded in 1854). The college is set on a hill, and I was privileged to be the Principal of an extraordinary community that believed in and practised generous orthodoxy.

We would often reflect, as a staff team, on what we thought we were doing with around 150 people, between their early 20s and early 60s, in this extraordinary 'vicar factory'. We knew that the instruction we offered was important. We also knew that spiritual and vocational formation—that deep, rich and almost inexplicable process whereby someone is gradually formed into a minister—took place in worship and over food as much as it did in the lecture theatre and seminar rooms. College life was a threefold, rhythmic process: we ate together; we worshipped together; we walked together in our common learning and pilgrimage.

But what was happening at a deeper level was, in some sense, much simpler: it was nothing less than the formation and cultivation of virtues. Those training for ministry learnt patience, kindness, self-control, humility, gentleness, graciousness and more besides. A seminary intensifies and grows character and virtues; the community cultivates goodness and faithfulness.

It is possible to be a minister and not very able at preaching or administration—possibly not a great leader or even a great pastor. But (and this is crucial) we do expect our ministers to be good people. By 'good', I mean full of goodness, brimming with the fruit of the Spirit. Psalm 15 sets out, in a few short verses, what we seek from each other and expect of ourselves. A blameless life; doing what is right; speaking the truth; not slandering; doing no evil. Being good, in other words. Being good, as God is good.

Luther, in his commentary on this psalm, exhorts us to turn away evil and hypocrisy, and hold fast to what is good. He reminds us that a faithful life will yield the fruits of the Spirit, and that these are the fruits that nourish the world and feed the soul. Indeed, as Luther said of Psalm 15, and as I would often say of Cuddesdon, there we are taught 'the truly good life, and true good works—the fruits of the Spirit and faith: to live blameless before God, to do right to the neighbour, and turn away from evil ways'.

5 Prophecy: the Midas touch?

Make no mistake: greed is a subtle, insidious sin. In questioning it, we are required to go deep into our hearts and minds, and to challenge our own motivations and desires. What really drives us? Why do we really want this or that for ourselves or for another?

I doubt that many people reading Psalm 97 bow down to graven images, or, as the psalmist has it, 'make their boast in worthless idols' (v. 7). But these verses can be read metaphorically. Our word 'greed' can be traced back to early Saxon times. It means a 'desire' or 'hunger', but one that has become a craving. It suggests that the very things we long to consume may, instead, consume us. This is the origin of folk fables like the story of Midas, who longs that all he touches might turn to gold.

Think, next, of the corporation that longs for global dominion, the institution that longs for a top international accolade, the person who craves recognition. Such things can be fine to aspire to, but, in excess, the greed that they produce corrupts all other relationships, distorting our humanity and society. Psalm 97 says that all this will melt before God; the dross will be consumed in the fire. Luther comments that 'he brings low all holiness, all wisdom, power, and whatever is great so that they might be holy, wise, great and powerful through Christ alone'.

We need to remember the subtlety of 'spiritual greed'—a desire for gifts that will seem worthy but in fact only promote us in the eyes of others. There can be a kind of distorted Christian greed—a desire for perfection that leads to false elevation and draws us away from wisdom; a longing to be 'holier-than-thou', which clouds the judgement of the person pursuing the path of righteousness.

Like Midas, we need to be watchful of our motives, lest we become too acquisitive and start to hoard. What we most desire to possess may become our possessor, our object of idolisation and worship. We can be trapped by unconstrained desire, by hunger that has no discipline. It imprisons us. 'Seek first his kingdom and his righteousness,' says Jesus (Matthew 6:33, NIV). And don't seek to possess anything, either; rather, let God possess you.

6 Gratitude: giving thanks in all circumstances

Psalm 30

We live in a world that seems largely secular, yet curiosity about higher things—God, mystery, transcendence—is the normal and natural state for humanity. Ironically, it is indifference to God and mystery that has to be learnt and cultivated. The haunting immanence that is the presence of God is among us and around us. The true light has come to the world.

So the writer of Psalm 30 continues to praise God and give thanks. The psalmist does not let go of the faithfulness of God in the midst of darkness and denigration, but proclaims that God's favour is 'for ever'. Luther adds that this psalm gives thanks for redemption from 'high spiritual afflictions'. The gratitude is rooted in the security of God's comfort and consolation.

The philosopher Alain de Botton tells us that thanksgiving is part of the fundamental core of faith. One of the differences between religious and secular lives, he says, is that religious people say 'thank you' all the time—when eating, going to bed or waking up; for this day; for life. Why does the secular world tend not to say 'thank you'? Possibly because to live in a state of gratitude is also to embrace our human vulnerability. De Botton says that when we feel grateful, we accept that we are indeed at the mercy of events and the people around us—even our foes. We acknowledge that our grand plans for our lives sometimes run aground.

But this need not lead to despair. We thank God for small mercies, even if we have nothing more to wonder at than the scent of a flower or a beautiful evening sky. To say 'thank you' for food or drink, or just some common courtesy, keeps us open to our dependency on others and to our own fallibility. As de Botton says, a person who remembers to be grateful is more aware of gift, chance and events, and is readier to meet with the tragedies that are awaiting us all down the road.

So we end our week with the psalmist, in gratitude—for all that God has given us, for what God has withheld and, above all, for God's faithfulness, favour and unceasing graciousness. As C.S. Lewis once said, in heaven we might spend an eternity thanking God for the prayers he didn't grant us, not just the ones he did. God is faithful.

Guidelines

Luther nailed his colours—his newfound theological and spiritual convictions—to the door of the church at Wittenberg. In his day, the church doors functioned as noticeboards, and his 95 theses, therefore, were simply serving notice. But notice of what, exactly?

Because we read history from the vantage point of our own era, we might sometimes assume that we understand Luther's agenda better than he did. In truth, we do not. Luther put up a notice, and, like all notices, it required attention. Luther wanted us to sit up and take note—to alert us to something we needed to pay attention to.

Luther's readings of the Psalms are rooted in his conviction that scripture has a 'natural sense'—that because God has chosen to speak to us plainly, we should be able to comprehend something of the God who has chosen to reveal his love and purpose for us. To be sure, God is mysterious and inscrutable, and no mortal can ever fully comprehend the fullness of God. But (and this was one of Luther's key insights) God has chosen to reveal himself through Christ. The God who was hidden from our eyes has made himself known to us. Reading the scriptures, faithfully, prayerfully and attentively, helps us to see the God who is beyond sight.

Luther's attention to the scriptures, and especially the Psalms, testifies to a God who wants his love and purposes for our lives to be seen and known. God does not leave us in darkness and ignorance. God draws us into light and knowledge. So our spiritual awareness grows as we dwell on God's word; we begin to see and sense God's life in ours, fashioning us more into his image.

For centuries, the prayers of the church have been rooted in the Psalms, because each and every day brings fresh trials and encounters to engage with. We encounter hope and despair, healing and hurt, light and dark, sadness and joy. The Psalms say—in many voices but ultimately in one beautiful symphony—that God is with us wherever we are. No matter what has befallen us, or what we might have become, God never leaves us or forsakes us. He abides in our everyday lives, so we might live with him for eternity.

1 Gratitude: thanks in adversity

Psalm 124

Luther classes Psalm 124 as one of thanks and gratitude, but I am tempted to say, 'by the skin of its teeth'. Part of the art of discipleship is discovering God in the uncomfortable, refusing the path of contentment and learning to turn again to Christ. One of Jesus' most significant (but harsh) times before his ministry was in a wilderness of hills—and he was led there by the Spirit.

In this psalm, there is a palpable sense of fear and dread. The psalmist, writing on behalf of the people, hints at threats: anger, desolation, being 'swallowed up'. Indeed, the same kind of 'flood' that once swept the marauding Egyptians away and so delivered the Israelites now threatens to engulf those who were once redeemed. The 'torrent' and the 'raging waters' (vv. 4–5) threaten to overwhelm God's people. But it is at precisely this point of threat and danger that the psalmist and the people turn to God. For God will hear the cry of his people: he will not forsake his own.

So to encounter God's redemption here requires a bit of a gamble—a genuine risk of commitment. It needs *movement* from us—a journey like a pilgrimage, perhaps, or time in solitude, to find our connection with God again.

Yet none of this *need* be done in total isolation. It's true that we may meet God alone, for we are made for togetherness with God. But we are also made to be with each other. Reconciling ourselves to our mutual interdependence is the key; this cannot guarantee immunity from suffering, but it does offer assurance in its midst. Deep commitments to God and others that grow in time and space can enable people to face the fickleness of life, holding them together in love.

You could say that the psalm, plainly put, tells us, 'You'll never walk alone.' The psalmist sees that we are in this together. Indeed, even when we are confronted by enemies, as Luther comments on this psalm, God will protect and rescue. Carefully, attentively, covenantally, God is there for *you*. None of that removes the reality of pain or evil and all their attendant fears. But it does suggest that if we are prepared to journey as a body—a group, a church, or even perhaps a nation—looking up to God and looking out for others, then 'our help is in the name of the Lord' (v. 8).

2 Comfort: God's protection

Luther's commentary on Psalm 121 stresses its comfort. More importantly, perhaps, it stresses that God is still with us, even when we might not sense his presence.

An analogy may help here. Most people, at some time or other, take out an insurance policy. Insurance exists because we are uncertain about the world in which we live, and we need some sense of protection. But it also plays on our fears. It's a case of 'can't live with it, can't live without it'. As one wag put it, 'In every insurance policy, the big print giveth, and the small print taketh away.'

In today's psalm, the print is big. The type of insurance on offer seems, implausibly, fully comprehensive, and with no strings attached. 'He who keeps Israel will neither slumber nor sleep' (v. 4); 'The sun shall not strike you by day, nor the moon by night. The Lord will keep you from all evil' (vv. 6–7). These promises seem to offer 24-hour protection—a policy well worth investing in. Is there a catch, then? Some small print, perhaps, lurking in the text, that might make you think twice before signing on the dotted line?

Psalm 121 is described as 'A Song of Ascents'. This is quite significant, because the song is looking *forward* to God's protection; it is more about what is to come than about the here and now. As we press on towards truth and God, so we encounter the living reality of God's abundance and comprehensive love.

In other words, this is a psalm about assurance, not insurance. Luther says, 'Although it appears as though God sleeps or slumbers, that we are struck down by the sun by day and moon at night, yet it is not so—though we may think it and feel it.' In my experience, God does not habitually stoop down to stop us stubbing our toe, or shade us from sunburn during a holiday in some Mediterranean resort. God respects our freedom too much to interfere in the details of our lives in that way. Doubts, suffering, evil, accidents—and insurance claims—are part of the world in which we live.

Prayer does not allow us to sidestep these problems. Instead, it acts as a help and comfort through them, for life is a journey in which we have to take the rough with the smooth, and discover the art of finding God in both.

3 Prayer: my cup runs over

This psalm is arguably one of the most unusual. It is frequently used in both weddings and funerals as a reading or hymn. If you think about it, we have few other hymns that would work in both contexts. For Luther, Psalm 23 combined thanks and prayer, and it offered promises of assurance in both feasting and famine. So the psalm also instructs us on the goodness of God. As Luther says, 'the faithful shepherd leads [us] to fresh grass and cool water'.

In Daniel Hardy and David Ford's seminal book *Jubilate: Theology in praise*, the authors start with a teasing question: 'What is the biggest or most fundamental problem facing the church today?' We'd all have answers to that question! But Hardy and Ford assert that the biggest problem facing the church is 'coping with the overwhelming abundance of God'.

The idea that we are struggling to cope with God's overwhelming abundance might come as a surprise, but this is just what Hardy and Ford want to confront us with. At the heart of the gospel is a God who can give more than we can ask or desire, and gives without counting the cost.

God gives in almost immeasurable portions: our cup runs over; the nets burst; we receive a hundredfold; he comes that we should have abundant life; the manna falls; the spring rises; the desert blooms. The scriptures testify to a God who blesses richly and abundantly.

The psalmist prays and gives thanks to God for this abundance of life. Although his confidence may seem overstated, it is rooted in three key convictions. First, God is always with us, even in the valley of the shadow of death. Second, God will lead us in dark and difficult times; his rod and staff are with us. Third, goodness and mercy will follow us.

Our prayers are rooted in the understanding that God will be with us, through whatever shadows or valleys we encounter. But we are not offered a detour. There is no way around the difficulties we face in life. Rather, faith offers a way through these things. So, as we face the challenges and opportunities ahead, we step out in trust and in hope. God is with us.

4 Instruction: make a joyful noise

Psalm 100

Christianity is a singing faith. We cannot do justice to our religion simply by speaking well, believing right or doing good. We sing. And when we sing, parts of our heart, mind and body that are often not used begin to offer something to God, and to one another, that speech and actions alone cannot achieve. When we sing, we stand, sit or kneel differently; we pray differently; we breathe differently.

The Christian who sings, said Augustine, prays twice. Singing is one of those activities in which we can't easily hold back. We give our all as our lungs and mouths open in praise. Not everyone can pray or speak lucidly, but most can sing with gusto. Few can play a musical instrument with beauty and precision, but everyone can make a noise in celebration. As Luther comments, this psalm 'calls on the entire world to be joyful, to praise, and to give thanks'.

Jean Vanier, the founder of L'Arche, says that God became small in our world in order to teach us to love and be open to those who are overlooked. Through Vanier's friendship with a priest named Thomas Philippe, he became aware of the plight of thousands of people with developmental disabilities, often shut away in institutions. Vanier sought to set them free to live in communities where they could express themselves more fully. The L'Arche Community is often known for its singing, because the God of tenderness, who loves us, raises us up so that we can all be instruments of his praise.

God is beyond our highest conceptions of the world, vast as it is. And yet (and this is the beauty of God) he has an eye and heart for detail. No sparrow falls, not one hair of your head is lost, without God noticing. We are God's. He made us. We are his people, and sheep of his pasture. We count to God, and we are counted.

Psalm 100 is a celebration of steadfastness, and, for Luther, it was a pivotal psalm of instruction. It simply tells of us God's love and tells us how to respond: sing; make some noise. God's grace is celebrated as an eternal kingdom, and so all nations are bidden to come and make a joyful noise. Singing and celebration are the right responses to God's love and mercy poured out on us. God is steadfast. God is good. God is faithful. His love endures for ever.

5 Prophecy: the true king

Psalm 45

Luther regarded Psalm 45 as pivotal, stating very clearly in his commentary that it speaks of Christ as a king. For him, it was a prophecy, foretelling the coming of the eternal king, who is Christ, and the bride, who is the Church. Luther comments that the psalm 'proclaims that the Old Testament shall come to an end'.

The emergent kingship of Christ, of course, is double-edged. Christ was mocked and crucified as king of the Jews. But, as Jesus makes clear throughout the Gospels, he is to be found in the lonely, the persecuted, the hungry, the scorned and the victimised. So Christians are first and foremost to be seekers of Christ the King in the people and places that the world habitually rejects. It is in loving the unloved and unseen that we begin to meet our maker.

Luther believed that this psalm pointed to the two great commandments: love the Lord your God with all your heart, soul and strength, and love your neighbour as yourself. The gospel has its heart set on raising up the fallen, the shunned and the oppressed. We therefore need to be ready to offer love to those who ache and long for a truly human life.

True religion is love, not reward. It is in giving that we receive, and in dying that we are born. During World War II, a Romanian Christian was imprisoned at Belsen. He prayed in secret—that he might respond to the call of love. He found himself spending time in the camp with the sick, the starving, the diseased, the dying and the betrayers—all those who were shunned by others. As the camp drew close to liberation, someone came to see the Romanian and said, 'I see how you live here. Tell me about the God you worship.' The Romanian replied, 'He is like me.'

Few of us could ever reply, 'He is like me.' Yet the call to discipleship remains compellingly simple: to be like him. We are called to love one another as he loves us, to bear fruit that will last, and to love those who have no one else to love them. As Jesus said, 'Truly I tell you, just as you did it to one of the least of these… you did it to me' (Matthew 25:40). Christ's kingship is one of sacrifice and service. Behold the servant-king.

6 Gratitude: God with us always

This is one of our best-loved psalms. It is a reminder that before we existed, God knew us, and that in the present and future there is no place where God will not be with us. Luther affirms, 'Whether the psalmist stands, walks, sleeps, or wakes—yes, even in his mother's womb, before he was made—God has been with him as he was being formed and will be with him as long as he lives.'

In the exquisite novel *The Boy in the Striped Pyjamas*, by the Irish writer John Boyne, and the no less beautiful retelling of the story in Max Herman's film of the same name, we encounter eight-year-old Bruno and his family leaving Berlin, during World War II, to live near the concentration camp where his father has just become commandant. Unhappy and lonely, Bruno wanders out behind his house one day and meets Shmuel—a boy in striped pyjamas who lives behind the barbed wire fence.

The boys become friends—an unlikely friendship, indeed—and play games through the wire. Eventually, Bruno finds a way of getting inside the camp to be with his friend. But in order to really fit in, he asks to put on the striped pyjamas worn by all the inmates. Shmuel finds him a spare set; Bruno quickly dresses like Shmuel and sneaks into the camp. Before they go back to the hut, Shmuel asks, 'Are you sure about this… are you sure you want to do this?' Bruno replies, 'There is no place I'd rather be, and no one I'd rather be with.'

This little scene says all you really need to know about Psalm 139, for God, in the ministry of Jesus, says, 'There is no place I'd rather be, and no one I'd rather be with than you.'

The psalmist is at peace and thanks God. God is not only Lord, but he will never abandon us. The mystics say that if God has one weakness, it is his heart: it is too soft. God cannot fail to love us. He does not know how to forget us. God cannot abandon his people. So we can take refuge in the God who *chooses* to abide with his people and love them. There is no place that God would rather be than with us. He abides with us. God is Emmanuel.

Guidelines

Luther read the Psalms as devotional Christian texts. His identification of a fivefold typology—gratitude, comfort, prayer, instruction and prophecy—was not meant to constrain the way we read them. It was, rather, his attempt to direct us to use them prayerfully, in corporate worship and in private devotion. Luther believed that the Psalms, like other parts of the Old Testament, prepared the way of the Lord: they spoke of the Christ who was to come. Luther's belief that the Psalms therefore foreshadow or echo the Lord's Prayer and the ten commandments should not surprise us. His view of the scriptures was symphonic, in the sense that the many notes and instruments combine to produce a greater harmony. The heart and mind need to be open to God, however, if we are to hear the notes and chords that God strikes through a verse or sung psalm.

The Christian church has used the psalms for its devotions since earliest times. That is because there is a beauty, rawness and honesty in their writing. Sometimes we are caught by the soaring hymns of praise, at other times by the cries of utter desolation. All human life is there, and God is woven in, under and above each psalm. The steadfastness and faithfulness of God, time and again, shines through the text.

The Psalms remind us that God does not deal with us on the basis of our potential, or as we might deserve. He meets us as and where we are, with the love, compassion and tenderness that Luther preached. The steadfast love of God is ever-new, and it is unfailing. We all stand before God in need. Luther knew that, no matter how far from God we may feel or however much we might despair, the Psalms, taken as a whole, testify to one of the great gospel truths. By God's free grace, we are saved.

FURTHER READING

Martin Luther (trans. Bruce Cameron), *Reading the Psalms with Luther*, Concordia, 2007.

Daniel Hardy and David Ford, *Jubilate: Theology in praise*, DLT, 1984.

Martyn Percy, *Thirty-Nine New Articles: An Anglican landscape of faith*, Canterbury Press, 2013.

Ben Quash, *Abiding*, Bloomsbury, 2012.

Martin Laird, *Into the Silent Land: The practice of contemplation*, DLT, 2006.

Luther on prayer

At an important level, the European reformers were pastoral at heart. Beyond all the polemics, politics and proliferation of the period, the reformers sought the good of those to whom they preached and for whom they wrote. As pastors and teachers they used the Bible and spiritual direction to instruct others on how to find their salvation in a gracious God, and how to engage with and experience God through Jesus Christ.

In that pastoral context, there was certainly no shortage of published works on prayer. Many of the reformers wrote on the subject, and all of them preached on it in their systematic teaching through books of the Bible. They all emphasised the sovereignty of God, his fatherhood, the central significance of Jesus Christ, the pivotal position of the Lord's Prayer and the importance of obedience, faith, hope and certainty in the supplicant. As we will see in the next six days, Martin Luther was no exception.

We're going to refer to three early pieces that Luther wrote on prayer: *An Exposition of the Lord's Prayer for Simple Laymen*, a sermon, and the longer booklet, *How One Should Pray* (or, *A Simple Way to Pray*). Notice the titles of the two published works: one is 'for simple [that is, untrained] laymen', and the other, written initially for Luther's barber, is 'a *simple* way to pray'. These are not theological treatises; they are pastoral guides, designed to help people to pray.

So, as we look at the biblical passages (all chosen because they demonstrate something of what Luther was about), we'll pick up some comments from the reformer that will aid us and energise our devotions. As we go through the week, we might seek to be 'simple laymen and women' and learn from Luther, grateful for his insight.

Martin Luther was a trinitarian theologian. The whole of his theological work is premised squarely on that understanding. So the first four days acknowledge that fact by centring our attention on prayer and the Trinity. The next two days respect the fact that the reformer saw salvation in communal terms and that he was supremely a biblical scholar.

Quotations are taken from the New International Version of the Bible.

1 Prayer: God the Father and our trust

Matthew 6:5–15; 7:7–12

Beneath everything that Luther says about prayer is the foundational teaching that prayer is a privilege, given to us by our gracious Father: it is essentially relational. Jesus asserts the same. Notice, he speaks of 'your Father' and 'our Father' in today's two passages. Against the common practice of prayer as mere rote (6:7), Luther asserts that heartfelt prayer is an inner longing, a sighing, the desire of a child approaching its Father. In prayer, he insists, we put our confidence in the fact that the sovereign, holy God is for us, not against us (7:9–11). He is actually our gracious Father—'a friendly, sweet, intimate, and warm-hearted word'.

Luther uses the wonderful metaphor of a sack that we hold open before our Father, in which we receive more and more, the longer we hold it open, for the Lord in his mercy desires or even longs to give (6:11; 7:8, 11). It's no wonder he exudes confidence in his praying. Strangely, perhaps, but with some force, Luther states that we should say the concluding 'Amen' firmly. Not only has God heard our prayer but he himself has said his divine 'Yes' to it; he cannot disdain our faith-filled prayers. That is what 'Amen' means! Something of this confidence seems emphasised in Matthew 7:7–8, for example.

And so we trust God when we pray. That idea surely lies beneath the two passages in Matthew's Gospel that we have read today. Jesus teaches his disciples to pray to 'Our Father in heaven' (6:9); those who knock will find the door opened (7:7); the Father gives good gifts (v. 11). The reformer is grateful to God who 'unasked, unbidden and unmerited' has offered to be *his* God. 'How could we ever in all eternity thank him enough?' Luther rejoices. However, always aware of his own sin, in his comments on the Lord's Prayer ('Lead us not into temptation': 6:13), he asks, 'O dear Lord, God and Father, keep us fit and alert, eager and diligent in your word and service, so that we do not become complacent, lazy and slothful as though we had already achieved everything.'

Humility, faith, enthusiasm, love and, above all, trust characterise Luther's praying to his heavenly Father.

2 Prayer: God the Father and our obedience

Exodus 20:1–7

Because God loves us, in prayer we trust him, says Luther. We saw that yesterday. Luther also speaks of prayer as obedience: 'You should pray and you should know that you are bound to pray by divine command.' Again, 'I have been commanded to [pray] and as an obedient person I must do it.' This isn't something we tend to stress today (perhaps we should), but evidently it was important to Luther. Where does he get the idea from?

The reformer attaches prayer to the second commandment: 'You shall not misuse the name of the Lord your God' (v. 7). He insists that if we are not to misuse God's name, we are *required* to use it in adoration: that is the positive flipside of the negative commandment. We might, at first, find this rather strange. We sometimes want prayer to be spontaneous and relational, not directed by rules. However, it's clear from Exodus that the commandment is underpinned by the relationship that the Lord has with his people. Exodus 20:2 speaks of his saving work for the Israelites. God repeatedly speaks of himself as 'the Lord *your* God'.

Luther speaks of our obedience to the law as demonstrating our relationship with God. We are obedient because God loves us and we respond to his grace. From this, three things follow. First, it gives added confidence to those who call on the Lord's name. Luther states that as God has demanded prayer, so he will graciously answer our obedient petitions. In typically forthright manner, he insists that God is therefore *bound* to answer his children! Second, if prayer is commanded, then we should not delay, thinking that after we've done something else we'll pray. Luther knows as well as we do, perhaps, that we probably won't return to pray, and then, he laments, 'nothing comes of prayer that day'. Third, although he shows some appreciation of the thought that everything we do in faith is prayer, Luther advises us 'not to break the habit of true prayer', by which he means those times of intentional fellowship with God. Our flesh is naturally 'disinclined to the spirit of prayer' and, if we consider everything to be prayer, then in the end nothing will be prayer. We will become lazy, doing nothing, praying nothing.

3 Prayer: Jesus Christ and our dependence

Ephesians 1:1–14

Because we are not naturally prone to pray, Luther encourages us, as preparation, to read the scriptures, particularly as they direct us to Jesus Christ. God's favour, a matter of undeserved grace and love, which we seek through prayer, has been gained solely through Jesus. In Christ we already have everything, says Luther. He alone is the basis on which we approach such a God.

This is the apostle Paul's emphasis as he writes to the Ephesians. We notice how often he claims Jesus Christ as central to the divine purposes and to their application. We're blessed in Christ (v. 3), chosen in him (vv. 4, 11), predestined in him (v. 5) and given grace through him (v. 6). We're redeemed and included, we have hope, and we receive the Holy Spirit in him (vv. 7, 12–13), all to the praise of his glory (v. 14).

Similarly, Luther never tires of proclaiming Jesus. Through his reading of Romans, he came to realise the centrality of Jesus Christ—helped as he was by his mentor, Joann von Staupitz, who advised him to cling to Jesus: 'One must keep one's eyes fixed on that man who is called Christ.'

He came to realise the central part that Jesus Christ played—that, while we remain sinners, Christ's righteousness is credited or freely given to those of us who believe. The wonderful image he often employs is of the blanket of Christ's sinlessness draped over the sinner, a blanket that covers or hides our sin. In this, God declares sinners to be what, in themselves, they are not—that is, righteous before God and able to stand before God. The heart of Luther's teaching, therefore, is that only in Jesus Christ has God given himself for us, utterly and without reserve.

God loves us in Jesus Christ! And Martin Luther loved Jesus Christ simply because, through him, we find access to the living God (as Paul states); through him we have salvation, through him we have life, and through him we have peace and a clear conscience. Staupitz' advice was all about Jesus. Luther's theology is all about Jesus. A biblical view of Jesus Christ reformed the young Luther. It energised him in his own spiritual life; it released him into spiritual freedom; it transformed him. That gospel change gave him humility, confidence and gratitude in prayer.

4 Prayer: the Holy Spirit and our experience

Paul is very clear in his letters that we experience the living God through his Spirit. The Christian faith is not a detached faith; we *experience* God. Having been brought into adoption through the Spirit, we cry 'Abba, Father' *by him* (v. 15)—and, according to James Dunn, the language used implies an experience of some intensity. Then, Paul assures us that the Spirit takes our wordless groaning and prays in tune with the divine will (vv. 26–27).

It sometimes surprises people reading the reformers, generally, that one of their repeated themes is that we actually experience God in our lives today. Perhaps reflecting Paul's words, in the context of his own thoroughly relational theology, Luther directs us away from an empty rote towards an experiential piety in which God may be the prime mover.

The context is Luther's challenge to be flexible in our praying, not to have every day's prayer identical with that of every other day. He wants us to avoid getting into a rut in our praying. He prefers that our hearts be stirred by what we read (see my comments in two days' time on Jonah and Acts 4), that our thoughts be guided by what we've thought through. So he encourages us to be flexible, lest we fall into a lazy habit of always saying the same things, in which there is no room for the Holy Spirit. In fact, it seems to me that the underlying element in his thinking—and one well worth contemplating in our own prayer lives—is that he refuses to be tied to rules and what we might call a bland 'normality'. Noticeably, he allows space for a genuine, intimate experience of the Holy Spirit working. He says, 'If in the midst of such thoughts [on reading the Lord's Prayer] the Holy Spirit begins to preach in your heart with rich, enlightening thoughts, honour him by *letting go of this written scheme*: be still and listen to him who can do better than you can. Remember what he says and note it well and you will behold wondrous things in the law of God' (emphasis added).

This calls for attentiveness, eagerness to hear the divine voice, a readiness to alter form, courage to listen and a trust in the God of grace.

5 Prayer: the context and our fellowship

Hebrews 12:1–3, 18–24; Acts 2:42–47

The writer of Hebrews encourages those who read his letter by reminding them of the 'great cloud of witnesses' who have gone before in faith and hope but have not yet received the promise (v. 1; 11:39–40). Later, he reminds them of the even wider company—'thousands upon thousands of angels... the church of the firstborn... God... the spirits of the righteous made perfect... Jesus' (vv. 22–24). The company we keep is significant for our spiritual lives. Again, it is in the community of faithful believers that prayer takes place, along with teaching, fellowship and the breaking of bread (Acts 2:42).

So, context is important. Martin Luther knew this. In his honesty and openness, he speaks of times when he becomes 'cool and joyless' in prayer—blaming both his own flesh and the devil for that obstruction to devotion. It is, of course, quite heartening to know that the great German reformer found himself 'cool and joyless' in prayer, but not something that should encourage us to complacency! However, when he finds himself in this state, he says that he either enters a room on his own to read and to pray or, if the time is appropriate, he goes into the church 'where a congregation is assembled'. He finds either a quiet place in solitude (Matthew 6:6) or a community of Christians with whom to seek the Lord (Hebrews 10:25). When we pray, Luther insists, we should do so knowing that we stand with 'all devout Christians', with the whole of the Church (12:1), united in prayer before God's throne. Luther's conclusion is that God cannot disregard such prayers. But notice, incidentally, that by saying this he encourages us to do something about the problem immediately. There is a danger of neglect if we procrastinate.

Context is important, too, for the focus and shaping of our prayers. Luther almost invariably takes into account both the wider world and his immediate circumstances: peace, his prince, people in towns, those living on the outlying farms, the weather and his own household.

When we pray in Jesus' name, we do so together with all the saints on earth and in heaven. This wider, universal, seen and unseen context of our prayers gives us confidence, boldness, faith and a sense of eternal perspective.

6 Prayer: the Bible and our contemplation

In our reading from Jonah, the prophet prays for deliverance from inside the big fish. He employs ideas and words from the Psalms; even the structure of what he says reminds us of some well-known psalms, such as Psalm 34 and Psalm 118. (Compare Jonah 2:2 with Psalm 34:4, 6 and 17, for example.) The second passage, from Acts, shows the nascent church, fearful for its own life, meeting in an upper room, praying the words of Psalm 2:1-2, which are appropriate to the intimidating situation in which the church finds itself. These are not isolated incidents, of course. So, it seems that good and effective prayer is rooted in and sustained by scripture.

Luther suggests a method of praying that grounds our prayers in the Bible, a method that he calls 'a garland of four strands'. Through it, the supplicant contemplates the biblical passage as comprising four strands, as it were—like a rope made from four separate cords intertwined together for a single strength: instruction (or teaching), thanksgiving (or grateful praise), confession (or repentance) and prayer (or supplication).

Elsewhere, Luther speaks of these aspects using the image of four books: a school book, a song book, a penitential book and a prayer book respectively. He explains that, if he has time, he takes the passage of scripture, reads and rereads it aloud to himself, reading it with the head and with the heart, turning to the four strands of the garland, and asking himself four questions. What is the Lord seeking to teach me 'so earnestly' from this passage? What should I be grateful for on reading this portion of scripture? What sins shall I confess? What do I now need to pray for, to cry out to God for? His repeated reading of the passage encourages him to think through the implications of each strand, which, in turn, help to shape his contemplation of the text and enable him to pray in a more biblically engaged way.

If you have time, read one of today's two passages again, asking the four questions that the reformer suggests. The answers you give will help shape your prayer.

Guidelines

Eugene Peterson argues that when we pray, we are engaged in 'something eternal'. Martin Luther reminds us that this is indeed the case. In prayer, he says, we connect with the triune God through the experience of the Holy Spirit, by the grace lavished upon us in Jesus Christ. Prayer is a privilege of the children of God. Importantly, it demonstrates that God is for us, not against us; that he is our Father, and that we are his sons and daughters.

Having said that, Luther is the first to admit his failings in this area. Sometimes he just doesn't feel like praying; sometimes he procrastinates, making other things paramount. The first thing that we might learn from him, then, is to be honest with ourselves about our own spiritual lives. Reflection on this is a good and profitable exercise. But Luther refuses to leave things there, advising, 'It is a good thing to let prayer be the first business of the morning and the last at night.'

Second, reading scripture is important to him. The Lord graciously speaks through his word, pointing us to Jesus Christ, encouraging our own piety, and rooting our prayers in the very words the Lord has spoken before us. Reading and rereading biblical passages beforehand is beneficial to prayer. Third, prayer opens the graciousness of God towards us. Like a father with his children, he cannot disdain faithful supplication, says Luther.

At this point, it might be useful to consider which of Luther's insights might help enrich your own experience and practice of prayer. This could be implemented for a month and re-evaluated to see if your spiritual life has been affected. Alternatively, you might like to attempt Luther's method of praying through a short biblical passage.

FURTHER READING

Michael Parsons, *Praying the Bible with Luther*, BRF, 2017.
Peter Matheson, *The Imaginative World of the Reformation*, Bloomsbury, 2000.
Eugene Peterson, *Working the Angles*, Eerdmans, 1987.

1 and 2 Thessalonians

Paul's correspondence with the early Christian community in Thessaloniki is widely acknowledged as the earliest Pauline material. While commentators disagree about whether to prefer the narrative chronology of Acts, Paul's own version of his travels or an attempt to unify the two, the point remains that the encouragement, exhortation and pastoral and doctrinal instruction of the two epistles represent an early stage of development in Pauline thought.

As a result of the apparent inconsistencies between the Lukan and Pauline timelines, it's unclear whether the correspondence was sent from Athens or Corinth. Additionally, scholars disagree over whether the authorship of the second letter belongs with Paul.

Thankfully, however, it is somewhat easier to appreciate the context into which these letters were speaking. The community in Thessaloniki was a fresh, vibrant expression of early Christianity. In Acts 17:4, we read that 'a great many of the devout Greeks and not a few of the leading women' took on the faith, and throughout 1 and 2 Thessalonians, Paul offers thanksgiving and acknowledgement of the strong witness of his fellow Christians.

A port city, strategically situated on the east–west Egnatian Way, Thessaloniki was replete with culture, thanks also to a rich Greek history combined with favourable Roman civil status. Cults of Roma, Dionysus, Sarapis and Cabiri (the local cult) were worshipped. The profound change from culturally expected religious behaviour, associated with conversion to Christianity, would have made Christians immediately identifiable.

Perhaps as a direct result of this, the community in Thessaloniki was experiencing persecution. Some commentators suggest that this persecution was compounded by personal grief. The Thessalonian church was under pressure and cracks were appearing in the community. We can detect division and disagreement about authority, right behaviour, ultimate purpose and relationship with the world.

Into this situation, the letters offer healing by providing pastoral encouragement, theological guidance and authoritative instruction. Citing the impact that the coming of the gospel has had on their lives, and the future hope that God offers them, Paul reminds the Thessalonians that to live well for Christ in the present requires a profound understanding of past, present and future.

Quotations are taken from the New Revised Standard Version of the Bible.

1 Faith lived out

One of the joys and challenges of moving into management or leadership is the increasing number of opportunities to offer feedback. Good managers or ministers quickly discover that positive reinforcement of excellent behaviour is the very best way to strengthen and support healthy attitudes.

In a way, Paul's opening remarks to the Thessalonians are an act of positive reinforcement among the Christian community. By retelling their shared story and highlighting what faith looks like, lived out, he gives an enormous encouragement to these Christians under pressure.

Early in his thanksgiving (v. 3), Paul describes the Thessalonian activity with what will become a defining triptych of virtues: faith, love and hope. Note the close alignment of these intangible virtues with grounded behaviours. 'Work', 'labour' and 'steadfastness' express the invisible through action—and not just any action, but hard-fought, drudging habits that enflesh the godly virtues 'in our Lord Jesus Christ'.

John Chrysostom writes on this passage, 'What labour is it to love? Merely to love is no labour at all. But to love genuinely is great labour. For tell me, when a thousand things are stirred up that would draw us from love, and we hold out against them all, is it not labour?'

Elsewhere in the passage, Paul continues to pick up faith lived out as a topic for thanksgiving. 'Conviction' and 'imitation' (vv. 5–6) epitomise the response of the church to the message of the gospel. By this imitation of right living, the Thessalonians themselves have become an example for others to witness. There is power in the witness of this Christ-formed behaviour, with Paul's own interactions with the Thessalonians becoming a well-known and defining story in the region (v. 8).

Already in the correspondence, Paul is beginning to pick up themes of the parousia (v. 10), which has evidently become a topic for debate among the Thessalonian community. The 'steadfastness of hope' mentioned in verse 3, then, has both practical and eternal resonances. It is a present hope that steadfastly withstands current sufferings and persecution, and an eternal hope that looks forward to the fulfilment of the salvific work of God in Christ Jesus.

What underlying virtues might others trace back from our behaviours, personally and corporately? How easy do we find it to identify and celebrate faith lived out among our sisters and brothers? And how might the everyday challenges we face be helpfully re-examined with an eternal perspective?

2 An authentic witness

1 Thessalonians 2:1–12

Who has been a defining example of Christ for you, and why does their example stand out in your memory?

One hallmark of a credible Christian witness is authenticity. There is nothing quite so jarring as a person who says one thing and does completely the opposite. And there is nothing as magnetic as somebody whose words and behaviours are in alignment with each other, and with those of Christ Jesus.

As Paul reflects further on his ministry among the Thessalonian Christians, he emphasises the continuity between the behaviours of Silas, Timothy and himself and the message that they brought to the church. Their motivation was 'to please God' (v. 4), not to 'seek praise from mortals' (v. 6) or to make 'demands as apostles of Christ' (v. 7). They have 'worked night and day' (v. 9), giving of themselves because of their care for the Thessalonians.

Twice, Paul uses familial terms to describe this relationship. The nursing mother (v. 7) is a deliberate metaphor for self-sacrifice and costly generosity, while the father (vv. 11–12) urges, encourages and pleads with care. The apostolic role that Paul is describing combines a ministry of teaching with a ministry of nurture. The parental metaphors, of course, imply proximity and affection, but also continuity and demonstrability of behaviour. There is an implicit parallel with the prophetic image of Isaiah 49:15: 'Can a woman forget her nursing-child, or show no compassion for the child of her womb? Even these may forget, yet I will not forget you.' Paul's witness is not one of a 'one-hit wonder', but a nurturing, forming, demonstrable witness which is credible and brings authority.

In 1974, Pope Paul VI said that modern people 'listen more willingly to witnesses than to teachers, and if [they do] listen to teachers, it is because they are witnesses.' In an age that continues to be characterised by suspicion of authority, these words remain vital, 40 years after they were spoken.

How different might today look if you strove, with the help of God, to live with deep authenticity? What might it mean for you to be sacrificial in your motivations? And how might the words and behaviour of your own church be aligned in witnessing to the local community?

3 Jesus never promised it would be easy

1 Thessalonians 2:13—3:13

Paul's focus now changes from giving thanks and reminding the Thessalonians about the authority by which he instructs them, to directly encouraging them in their present sufferings.

While some commentators question the Pauline origin of 2:13–16, given the unique vocabulary and rhetoric used against 'the Jews', it is clear from what follows that the Thessalonians need to make sense of what it means to be Christian in a hostile climate. In verse 13, they are encouraged to remember that the basis of their faith is divine: they accepted it 'not as a human word but as what it really is, God's word'.

Paul recollects that the readers had been prepared for such hardships, citing his own experiences before arriving in Thessaloniki (2:2) and his prescient instruction when he was among them (3:4). The visible, distinctive behaviour of these new Christians, praised by Paul earlier in the letter, also entailed separation from worship practices associated with both religious and imperial powers. This distinction brought mistrust and persecution.

Paul, aware of the impact that such hostility can make, encourages the church by extending the horizon in view to the parousia (2:19), sending Timothy as an act of solidarity (3:2), and emphasising the encouragement that they have provided for him (3:7). In this way, he seeks to set their suffering in the context of a maturing faith, speaking to them with fraternal (2:14, 17; 3:7) and childlike (2:17) affection, as opposed to paternalistic instruction.

This progression from the 'nursing mother' and 'father' images employed earlier in the letter is entirely consistent with Paul's approach in emphasising the Thessalonians' maturation (and associated suffering) as a joyful consolation. This hallmark of true witness brings a kind of parity to the relationship.

For all Christians who are inviting others to follow Jesus, there is an inherent tension in describing the profound joy of a renewed life and yet the challenge that genuine detachment from the world's values brings. As my former bishop used to repeat, 'Jesus never promised that it would be easy.'

How do we prepare others and ourselves for encountering the challenges of a life lived in contradiction to the people around us, and how do we encourage and console others in the midst of their struggles?

4 Holiness and love

1 Thessalonians 4:1–12

Have you ever had a crisis of confidence? What helped you to be galvanised and push forward, despite your circumstances?

I remember receiving a letter from my parents while I was volunteering overseas as a lay missionary, surrounded by anxieties in the team I was working alongside and troubles in the situation where I was ministering. Their letter was exactly what I needed to enable me to 'dig deep' and continue in the path that the Lord had led me in.

We can imagine that the Thessalonian community felt hemmed in. Perhaps many were losing confidence and were tempted to abandon the way of life on which they had set out in earnest. So, Paul moves into an exhortation of the believers, both reminding them of the teaching that they already know and encouraging them to practise this teaching increasingly, in order to grow in holiness. Holiness and love of others are the two prominent themes. We can situate these qualities within a context where permissiveness was a cultural expectation. That counter-Christian sentiment may have stretched the outward-looking 'agape' love (v. 9) of the Thessalonian community to breaking point.

After encouraging the community in their pursuit of holiness, Paul offers them three motivational reasons for right living. First, God's impending judgement should spur them on (v. 6). Second, it is the call of God that they are answering while living chaste lives (v. 7). Third, the Holy Spirit has been given to the believers (v. 8). Paul uses rhetoric here to locate their temporal struggles in an eternal and everlasting framework.

Given the preceding focus on an authentic witness (ch. 2), it's clear that Paul, Silas and Timothy have authority to exhort the community to live simply (vv. 10–12). Their own ministry has been underwritten by toil 'night and day' (2:9); thus, the direction given in 4:11 carries the sense of both verbal and physical demonstration.

How might you hear this word of exhortation from God today? Where do you need encouragement to continue in the path you have begun, and how might your daily struggles be brought to God in the light of your eternal journey?

5 Children of the day

1 Thessalonians 4:13—5:11

This section of the correspondence is of significance to both Paul and the community at Thessaloniki. Paul addresses a fundamental issue that has been highlighted since the return of Timothy, and draws attention to its importance by opening with the Pauline phrase, 'We do not want you to be uninformed' (4:13).

His instruction about the parousia falls into two parts: he writes of what will happen to Christians who have died (4:13–18), and of when the day of the Lord will come (5:1–11). N.T. Wright suggests the helpful analogy of Christians meeting Jesus and bringing him back to their city (rather than of Christians disappearing to a heavenly realm) as a way to understand these two strands of thought.

We can assume that loss has been experienced in the community at Thessaloniki. Grief has been expressed, and Paul is keen to emphasise that the sorrow felt by Christians should not have the same character as the sorrow felt by others (4:13). This wrongly felt Christian sorrow centres on the privilege that the still-living are believed to have on the day of the Lord. Using mystical language ('by the word of the Lord', 4:15), Paul declares that the reverse will be true. In so doing, he preferences the Christian dead as the first to rise to life in Christ.

Having addressed the present grief felt by the community, Paul broadens the theme to address falsely reassuring apocalyptic teaching (5:3). By using prevalent images of light and darkness, Paul intertwines his theology of the end times with teaching on holiness and right living, to re-emphasise his earlier discourse in chapter 4. For Paul, the present reality and the future reality are both equally present in the lives of Christians, and this is how he can use the uncertainty of the end times as a certain opportunity for them to 'encourage one another' (5:11).

We see here also a repetition of the earlier triad of faith, love and hope (1:3; 5:8), allegorised in military attire (revisited, notably, in Paul's letter to the church in Ephesus). It is pertinent that hope here is again the distinguishing, third characteristic that can provide ballast for a community shaken by personal loss and corporate challenge.

How might you live differently today, confident in the hope that Paul describes? Do you consider yourself a 'child of the day'? How does an eternal perspective bring sharp focus to your daily concerns?

6 A faithful God

1 Thessalonians 5:12–25

As his correspondence with the Thessalonian Christians closes, Paul draws together some themes of the letter and addresses particular questions and behaviours that he knows to be relevant in the community—either from his own experience or from Timothy's report.

Within the final exhortations, we hear echoes of a call to unity (vv. 12–13), hard work (v. 14) and thanksgiving (v. 18), which have all been present in Paul's preceding chapters, and are attuned to the Thessalonian experience of faith lived out in the context of persecution.

Some commentators see verses 16–22 as an early form of practical discipleship training—memorable, pithy rules to live by. Joy undergirds these rules (v. 16) and is accompanied by prayer, attentiveness to the Spirit and right living.

By the time of Ignatius' Letter to Polycarp (the turn of the first century AD), Paul's encouragement to 'pray without ceasing' had become a fundamental hallmark of Christian ministry. The blossoming of this tradition over two millennia in such diverse manifestations as the Divine Office, the Jesus Prayer, charismatic glossolalia and 24/7 prayer demonstrates the captivating vision of Paul's instruction.

The theme of the parousia is picked up again at verse 23. Paul's concern in describing 'spirit and soul and body' is not to offer an argument about the constituent parts of a human, or to assert a bodily/spiritual resurrection, but to emphasise the holistic and total character of the life of attentiveness to the 'God of peace'.

Amid the multiplicity of concerns affecting the community in Thessaloniki, Paul's final theological assertion must have had significant resonance: 'The one who calls you is faithful, and he will do this' (v. 24). In some ways, the entire letter has been a celebration of the faithfulness of God. He has faithfully grown the Thessalonian community. He has kept the bonds of friendship and discipleship between Paul, Silas, Timothy and the community. He will be faithful both through persecution and at the end of time, and will faithfully complete the call in the lives of the believers.

What does it mean practically for us to recognise this faithful God whom Paul describes? How does God's faithfulness change the way in which we relate to others and the world around us? And how does it change the way in which we relate to God? Might there be an opportunity today to grow in our appreciation for a God who is faithful?

Guidelines

The idea of time is complex in the life of a Christian. From the opening chapters of Genesis to the closing words of Revelation, we are acutely aware of the continuous, unfolding nature of God's revelation to humanity. Yet this flowing tide is punctuated by moments of the defining 'now', most notably in the incarnation, death, resurrection and ascension of Christ Jesus.

Our own sense of time is both fleeting and everlasting, and we become less than we might be when we rigidly focus on the present or the eternal at the expense of the other. In our imitation and reflection of the divine, we most fully capture the character of God when we view time in a balanced and holistic manner. It's this balance that 1 Thessalonians can speak to in our lives as Christians in the 21st century. Our present realities matter. Paul was deeply concerned for the people he knew and loved, and for the challenges that they faced. He was practical and affirmative, citing his own experience of the reality of life in Thessaloniki.

Yet Paul also speaks confidently in the future tense. He is able to see today in the light of tomorrow, without being so heavenly minded that he is of no earthly use.

Certainly, Paul's correspondence has become known for its vivid familiarity with the parousia, but it should perhaps be better known for its ability to translate that future vision into earthly living now—characterised by perseverance under pressure, practising thankfulness and seeking holiness.

As we seek to reflect on the whole of this letter, it might be useful to consider our own relationship to time.

- Do I tend to live in the past, the present or the future when I am with others?

- Do I tend to live in the past, the present or the future when I am with God?
- What does an eternal perspective bring to the problems that I face today?
- What does an eternal perspective bring to the problems that the church and society face today?

1 Steadfastness and faith

2 Thessalonians 1:1–4

The themes of this second letter to the church in Thessaloniki correlate closely with those of 1 Thessalonians. Even in these earliest verses, we hear linguistic echoes of the earlier correspondence and find familiar themes of mutual upbuilding in the context of persecution.

Although there is a debate in contemporary scholarship over the exact authorship of this letter, it is received within the Pauline corpus and helps to demonstrate the development of thought and the interplay of ideas around the parousia in particular, which was such a vivid and immediate issue among the persecuted Christians of the day.

Accordingly, we find two virtues recurring early on, as the writer gives thanks for the Thessalonians—steadfastness and faith. The faith noted in verse 4 is not merely received faith or belief, but a lived-out faith that endures adversity and suffering. It is surely because of this endurance that the brothers' and sisters' faith is growing abundantly (v. 3). Steadfastness is a critical virtue for the Thessalonians, given their situation as persecuted believers; it also underpins their understanding of themselves as imitators of Christ. As the letter concludes, so they will be encouraged that Jesus himself is steadfast (3:5), and the mutuality and reciprocity of this steadfastness is itself a prophetic symbol of Jesus.

There can be a danger in contemporary Christian life in the West that our experience of faith becomes therapeutic or transactional. In certain cases, the good news of Jesus can be reduced to a no-obligations happiness provider, or, elsewhere, as a kind of quasi-commodity to add to the suite of family assets. But the lives of countless followers of Christ today demonstrate clearly that faith can become most fully fledged when it is neither comfortable nor comforting. A steadfast faith transcends emotions and seasons and is a gift from God, honed by challenge and cultivated in the company of others.

Throughout the rest of the letter, the writer will continue to explore what this steadfast faith should look like in eschatological and ecclesiological terms. Here, however, there is simply celebration of the witness that a growing faith provides for the wider Christian community in the region.

Do you know anybody who is suffering for their faith? How might your own faith be strengthened in adversity? And what particularly might it mean for your faith to be steadfast today?

2 Judgement

2 Thessalonians 1:5–12

It has become something of a spiritual cliché that opposition is a sure signifier that we are following a godly path. While this might be an overused piece of guidance, there are plenty of biblical and ecclesiastical precedents that affirm the principle.

Here, the letter takes up this argument, citing the persecutions and afflictions described in verse 4 as evidence of the Thessalonians' eternal reward. For the writer, there is a demonstrable link between suffering for the kingdom now and belonging to the kingdom in the future.

Equally certain is the analysis of the future adjustment in the balance of suffering. The repetition of 'affliction' in verses 4, 6 and 7 emphasises how those who are currently afflicting will become those who are afflicted themselves. This cosmic readjustment is, of course, also evidence of God's right judgement and justice.

The vision of the parousia presented in verses 9–10 is more evocative and sensory than the more sober and functional presentation in 1 Thessalonians 4. Fire, angels, vengeance, punishment and destruction all borrow heavily from the apocalyptic literature of the Hebrew Bible (see especially Daniel 7; Isaiah 2 and 63) and Jewish intertestamental writings (see especially the Enoch tradition). In contrast to 1 Thessalonians, where the focus of Paul's reference to the coming of Jesus is on present Christian behaviour, here the emphasis is on future retribution and vindication.

The vivid description segues into a prayer for the Thessalonian Christians in verses 11 and 12. Again, a connection is drawn between activity ('good resolve and work of faith') and its perfection by God's power, with the ambition that the 'name' (meaning the very person or essence) of Jesus will be glorified.

Perhaps unsurprisingly, glory is a theme that weaves through this section of the letter. Glory is the quality of the Lord's 'might', power and strength (v. 9), and the future act of glorifying goes hand in hand with marvelling by God's saints (v. 10); yet this transcendent glory of Christ is seen in the lives of the believers, and even transferred to the believers as they find themselves in him (v. 12). Once again, the eternal and expansive fuses with the immediate and personal.

Where might you discern challenge, in your own life or the lives of those around you, resulting from following God's call? How might this suffering be an opportunity to discover more about the glory of God?

3 Lawlessness and restraint

2 Thessalonians 2:1–12

It is worth pausing for a moment at this point to remind ourselves of the end-times expectations of both the letter's writer and its recipients. In 1 Thessalonians, Paul has already indicated the proximity of the coming of Jesus, in response to raw, immediate questions emanating from the community themselves.

There is no doubt that the communication of an apocalyptic vision (2 Thessalonians 1:5–12) and this instruction on the parousia (2:1–12) were of critical importance to the Thessalonian community, and were seen as deeply practical theology. The distance from the text that we feel today can mean we try to construct a coherent eschatological theory from these verses, but it may be a good exercise to feel them as theologically descriptive, evocative and full of implications for application today.

Standing dominant throughout this section is the 'lawless one' or 'man of lawlessness'. The revelation of this figure is a necessity before the day of the Lord can come. The expression 'man of...' denotes 'intimacy with...', in this case, with lawlessness or sinfulness. 'Rebellion' or 'apostasy' (v. 3) became a signifier of end times in intertestamental literature, after the persecutions carried out by Antiochus IV Epiphanes (175–164BC), and is the hallmark of the man of lawlessness.

Who 'the man of lawlessness' actually refers to is not known. He is an agent of Satan (v. 9), and his 'parousia' is accompanied by signs that parody the real parousia accompanying the day of Jesus Christ. These subverted accompanying signs include self-divinisation (v. 4), power, signs, lying wonders and wicked deception (vv. 9–10).

Throughout, though, it is clear that the power of the man of lawlessness (and, indeed, Satan) is flawed. Christ is forcefully declared triumphant over him (v. 8). He is not yet revealed because of an external restraining force, of which the Thessalonians are aware (v. 6) but we are not. The nature of this restraining force has been debated, with plausible suggestions including prayer, the archangel Michael, the Holy Spirit and the Roman Empire, but the critical point is that the Thessalonians can be sure that, ultimately, God their Father is in control.

The language of this passage—in terms of both God's control and Satan's activity—may jar on our ears. But how might today's world be helpfully narrated by this language? Who are the individuals, organisations or systems bringing deception and acclaiming self-divinisation? And how might our own activity be a restraining force for God's kingdom?

4 Belief and prayer

2 Thessalonians 2:13–17

I'm sometimes struck by the timing of the intercessory prayers that form part of the formal Sunday liturgy in my particular church tradition. Rather than beginning with these universal prayers (which might get the intentions 'off our chest' quicker) or ending with them (which might send us out mindful of a life of prayer), we pray roughly midway through the service, after our creedal affirmation and before the Eucharist. This serves to remind me that offering prayers and thanksgiving should be an informed response to the faith I profess, and that intercession connects what I believe with how I live.

Here, the letter moves into prayer and thanksgiving for a second time, now as a response to the vision and instruction that the Thessalonians have received. The thanksgiving clearly situates the Thessalonians in the plan and control of God, responding to the grand themes of apocalypse and parousia.

With this in mind, I prefer to read the NRSV's 'first fruits' in verse 13 with the alternative reading of 'from the beginning', as this sets the cosmic landscape of the Thessalonian call (notwithstanding that the Thessalonians weren't the first to hear the gospel). The situation of this call within the plan of God is a cause for prayerful joy.

The interplay between faith and prayer is emphasised by Paul's diversion from prayer in verse 15 to encourage the Thessalonians to hold on to their genuinely received faith. This, of course, also points to the context already mentioned earlier, in 2:2, where we read that confusion about the nature of the end times is being created by a profusion of sources claiming authority.

Note, too, in this short prayer the repetition of the Thessalonian theme of 'eternal comfort' being brought to the current situation, and of the resultant outworking of this eternal reality as the witness of 'every good work and word' (vv. 16–17). Once again, the eternal shouldn't be a vague, distant reality, but something that inspires and changes the way in which today is lived.

What different quality might your intercessory prayer take on today, as you are reminded of the eternal truths of your Christian journey? And how might you talk about your own call in the context of a universe-spanning narrative?

5   The urgency of the gospel

2 Thessalonians 3:1–5

In these verses, the Thessalonians are invited to respond to all that has been imparted to them by praying for Paul, Silas and Timothy in their missionary endeavour. Despite the reassurances of the previous chapter, both in terms of the timing of the last days and the long-term calling of the Thessalonians, the request here for prayer carries urgency: the phrase 'spread rapidly' (v. 1) could be translated literally as 'run'. Lest the Thessalonians forget, the missionary intent and imperative continues.

Elsewhere in the Pauline corpus, prayer is sought for deliverance (for example, Philippians 1:19; Romans 15:30–31), courage (Ephesians 6:19) and opportunity (Colossians 4:3–4). Here in 2 Thessalonians, the focus is upon growth of God's message, as well as rescue from wickedness. These issues were, of course, particularly resonant with the Thessalonian believers themselves, and the spiritual solidarity forged between Thessaloniki and the Pauline community is reinforced with prayer.

Reintroducing the theme of glorification (v. 1), Paul acknowledges the Thessalonians' own witness to the glory of the word of the Lord. In being asked to pray for others to experience the same glorifying experience of the gospel, the Thessalonians are implicitly praised once again for their own responsiveness and encouraged to persevere in their own openness to sanctification.

Much of this section echoes theological themes found in the first letter to the Thessalonians. The reminder that 'the Lord is faithful' (v. 3) repeats 1 Thessalonians 5:24—a message that would have found a home among a persecuted community who were struggling to make sense of their immediate and eternal destiny.

Similarly, here we also see a return of the three Pauline virtues that opened the very first section of 1 Thessalonians. In this instance, though, the virtues are used as divine descriptors rather than human responses to God's grace. The Lord is faithful (v. 3); God is loving (v. 5); Christ is steadfast (v. 5). So, the call of the Thessalonians is to embody the divine life.

What is your own sense of the urgency of the gospel? How do you combine a sense of God's unendingness and faithfulness with this urgency? And what does it mean to you for God to be full of faith, love and hope?

6 The danger of idleness

2 Thessalonians 3:6–18

As the letter draws to a close, we can expect some direct instruction on pastoral issues, and here the problem of idleness within the Thessalonian community is again addressed. Having been briefly mentioned in 1 Thessalonians 5:14, the behaviour has been implicitly challenged throughout both letters. But now the focus is far more deliberate and explicit.

The behaviour of Paul, Silas and Timothy is cited once again as both an example of enabling ministry ('that we might not burden any of you', v. 8) and an empowering example for imitation (v. 9). Moreover, an explicit personal teaching is now invoked (v. 10), bringing additional rhetorical force to the previous encouragement to 'hold fast to the traditions that you were taught by us' (2:15).

Idleness, then, is a deeply concerning pastoral issue for the Thessalonian community. But why?

Clearly, there is a practical dimension to the issue of idleness. The community is not able to operate as effectively as it perhaps could do. Indeed, 'busybodies' (v. 11) who are less confined by the rigour of work may begin to cause relational issues. Also, of course, once one portion of the community begins to feel resentment, then significant dysfunctionality becomes a major pastoral problem. It's presumably for this reason that the treatment of idlers should be so strong (vv. 14–15).

However, it may be that equally strong theological problems occur when idleness creeps in. Pragmatically, the more that people idle their time away awaiting an imminent parousia, the more the incorrect narrative of its immediate proximity (challenged in chapter 2) persists. Additionally, we get the impression that even if the end of the world were going to happen later today, Paul would still push for quiet working and practical witness. For the Thessalonian community, the key message of these letters is that eternity is a fixed and welcome horizon, but the only way of making sense of that horizon is to inhabit the here and now. To idle time away is to lose the sacred, salvific potential of this world in favour of the next.

What does idleness look like in our communities today? It may not be about people's work status; it may be about putting off commitments from the here and now. And what things in your own life do you feel you have a propensity to be idle about?

Guidelines

2 Thessalonians may be taken as an account of the forces of good and evil in the lives of Christians. While the letter doesn't seek to provide a worked-out theodicy, it looks at good and evil through the lens of the challenges, questions, experiences and behaviours of a practising community of believers.

The powers of evil currently afflicting the community, through persecution, will find the tables turned and their own affliction coming. Evil is personified in the man of lawlessness, and with the personification come self-glorifying attitudes and corrosive behaviours. Yet godly powers will overcome, and the attributes of godliness (faith, love and hope) are worked out in the lives of the Thessalonian community. But a seemingly benign behaviour, idleness, can contradict both the epoch-shaking narrative and the peaceable living of the community and thus reintroduce evil in its most tangible form.

This view of the corrosive nature of idleness has irrevocably shaped Christian and wider culture. The 'Protestant work ethic', the simplicity embraced by the Amish, the *opus dei* of the monastic communities, the philosophy of Simone Weil and the prophetic determination of Dorothy Day and the Catholic Worker Movement have all sought to identify work as a milieu to cultivate holiness. Yet, in our frenetic working world, which measures success by output and ministry by impact, we need also to redress a potential imbalance in our view of work: salvation comes not from work itself but from the God whom we meet in the midst of our work.

As we conclude our reading of both 1 and 2 Thessalonians, some questions which may be worthy of deeper consideration emerge:

- How does the eternal landscape of the kingdom of God impact the way I live in the here and now?
- Do I enact any behaviours (such as idleness) that limit or reduce the vision of God's eternal plan?
- What comfort and encouragement can I bring to those who are the most persecuted and oppressed Christians today?
- How can my own experience of faith, love and hope be enriched and refreshed anew by waiting for the God who is faithful?

FURTHER READING

Raymond Brown (ed.), *New Jerome Biblical Commentary*, Continuum, 2002.

Karl P. Donfried, *The Theology of the Shorter Pauline Letters* (New Testament Theology), Cambridge University Press, 1993.

Earl J. Richard, *First and Second Thessalonians* (Sacra Pagina), Liturgical Press, 1995.

Tom Wright, *Paul for Everyone: Galatians and Thessalonians*, SPCK, 2002.

God's Advent call

For many people, Advent is no longer a time of preparation but is the time when they celebrate Christmas; by the end of Boxing Day it is all over. For us as Christians, Advent has a twofold focus on remembering and celebrating Christ born as a baby, God made incarnate for all, and on being ready for Christ's glorious return in triumph.

The traditional Advent scriptures help us to keep this balance in mind. Some of the characters whose stories are told and whose writings are used can help us see more clearly how we must be not only Easter people but also Advent people, waiting, ready and prepared to make our homes in Christ.

The call of Advent is similar to the way the Baden-Powells put it in their original handbooks for Scouts and Guides:

> The Scout Motto is: BE PREPARED which means you are always in a state of readiness in mind and body to do your DUTY.

> The motto of the Girl Guides is 'Be Prepared'. Why is this? It is because, like the other Guides, you have to be prepared at any moment to face difficulties and even dangers by knowing what to do and how to do it.

The biblical characters we shall consider in the coming week bring a variety of challenges and encouragements to be prepared for the coming of Christ into our lives. Noah reminds us to be obedient, even when it seems crazy to do so. Isaiah reminds us to look forward and to follow in Christ's light. Jesse and David remind us who the Messiah is and how we must aspire to be like him in our hearts. John calls us to repent and be made clean. Joseph and Mary make a home for God, challenging us to do the same. Paul calls us to be like him, an ambassador for Christ and one of God's holy people.

Quotations are taken from the New Jerusalem Bible.

1 Noah says, 'Be prepared'

Matthew 24:37–44

Noah is the first character we shall consider in our Advent readings, and Matthew uses him to highlight the necessity for us to be prepared. It can be hard to go against what is expected of us by society (and, sometimes, other members of our churches) and do things that seem crazy in other people's eyes. Noah acted against the norms of his society to follow what God had called him to do—to build the ark. His trust in the Lord and his obedience are an example to us all.

We are told in Genesis 6:9 that Noah was 'righteous' and 'blameless'—a hard act to follow—and in this he foreshadows for us the person of Christ. Matthew urges us to stay awake and stand ready, for 'the Son of Man is coming' (v. 44)—the one who also is righteous and blameless. Unlike Noah's, however, Jesus' actions will save and restore the people, the whole world, once and for all. We are to prepare for his glorious return and be ready for it at all times.

At the time of Noah, people were going about their daily lives right up to the moment of the flood. It was business as usual; they were blind and deaf, neither looking nor listening for the voice of God (vv. 38–39). Similarly, when Christ returns, it will be swift and sudden and will come at an unspecified time and date. Matthew suggests that, at Christ's coming, the choices we have already made about how to live, what to believe and how to act will be the ones that determine our eternity. The text sharply reminds us that our decision for Christ is urgent and, like good Scouts and Guides, we must 'be prepared'.

The equivalent passages in Mark 13:33–37 and Luke 21:34–36 do not reference Noah but they take a similar tone to Matthew, exhorting us to prepare, to be alert and on our guard.

Like Noah, we are called to be righteous and blameless, to seek out mercy and forgiveness, to be instruments of justice and peace and to be builders of the kingdom of heaven. We are called not simply to buy presents, decorate our homes and feast together but to build our spiritual arks, to 'stay awake' (Matthew 24:42) and prepare for our 'homeland… in heaven' (Philippians 3:20).

2 Isaiah says, 'Walk in the light'

Isaiah 2:1–5

Isaiah is the next character from the Advent scriptures that we encounter. The words attributed to Isaiah here are among the earliest Old Testament prophecies, and Isaiah is arguably preeminent among the prophets.

As prophet to the nation and adviser to kings, Isaiah warned Israel of the judgement to come but also, in the book's later chapters (probably from a different original source), told of the coming king who would reign as a servant and 'bear the sin of many' (53:12).

In chapter 2, early in Isaiah's collected writings, we are looking at the end times again, a common Advent theme. In the 'final days' that Isaiah speaks of (v. 2), the glory of God will be unmistakable and irresistible. As readers of this passage in the times after Jesus' life, death and resurrection, we recognise the unmistakable and irresistible call that Jesus has had on our lives and can see how Christ is part of this glorious revelation.

Verse 3 exhorts us to meet God in the high and holy places. We are encouraged to come together, to go to the mountaintop to be close to where God dwells—the place of encounter, where the law and the person of God are revealed. This call urges us to seek out opportunities for worship, for retreat, for closeness with God. It demands an openness to be taught, to learn more about what it means to follow in his path and be a disciple. It asks for a willingness to be open to change.

As we walk in his path, in the light, we are equipped to be people of peace and unity (v. 4). We are enabled to be his disciples, to be covered in his dust, so that others may follow us. If we walk in the light, the way ahead is clear to us; we are unlikely to stumble and fall as we will see any hazards as we approach them.

Verses 4 and 5 speak of peace and unity among nations. The enactment of God's law through his judgement and word is the harbinger of this peace and unity, and it calls us to live as if unity has already been achieved while doing all we can to make it so.

3 Jesse and David plant a tree

Isaiah 11:1–10

This messianic poem describes the key characteristics of the coming Messiah.

First, the Messiah will be of Davidic stock, Jesse being the father of King David. Some scholars suggest that by specifying a line back to Jesse, beyond David, Isaiah is making an implied criticism of the Davidic kings, but this is not our focus here. Matthew's Gospel breaks up the genealogy of Christ into three parts, in which the first and second parts hinge on Jesse and David (Matthew 1:6), while Luke 1 and 2 mention the Davidic line numerous times with reference to Jesus.

'The spirit of the Lord shall rest on him' takes us back to the 'divine wind' in Genesis 1:2, which brought forth the first creation. This same 'wind' or 'spirit' is within the Messiah, who will bring about a new creation. All creation owes its life to this one Spirit, the breath of God, and the same Spirit gives the patriarchs and prophets God's word to speak. The same Spirit is the Messiah's, which he freely breathes out on to the disciples (John 20:22) so that they will, in turn, share it with all.

Verse 3, 'He shall not judge by what his eyes see', again reminds us of the choosing of Jesse's son to establish the messianic line (1 Samuel 16:7).

Verses 4–5 tell us that the Messiah will establish an integrity of law and justice on earth which mirrors that of heaven. In Isaiah's day, the kingdom of Judah was surrounded by hostile nations and had itself become corrupt. His prophecy of the Messiah strikes at the heart of Judah, demanding righteousness, justice and faithfulness, particularly towards the poor and outcast. God calls forth from us too this active response towards others.

Our rebellion against God, as told in the Eden story in Genesis 3, broke the harmony between humankind and the rest of creation. In verses 6–9, Isaiah envisions its restoration with the coming of the Messiah. The Messiah will bring peace to all creation, and Eden will be restored.

Verse 10 takes us back to Jesse and points us to Christ as a 'signal'. We are called to seek him out and see his glorious dwelling place. This raises our minds heavenwards, to our promised eternal resting-place, our glorious heavenly homeland (Philippians 3:20).

4 John prepares the way

In Matthew's Gospel, the account of the adult life of Jesus begins with John the Baptist and his proclamation of the kingdom of heaven. The phrase 'kingdom of heaven' rather than 'kingdom of God' is particular to Matthew's writing. He uses it in deference to the Jewish reverence for the name of God. John's message about repentance, preparation, the proximity of the kingdom of heaven, baptism and the coming Messiah, along with his scathing attitude to the Pharisees and Sadducees, sets the tone for the rest of Matthew's Gospel.

The repentance that John the Baptist proclaims in verse 2 is *metanoia*, a Greek word meaning a total conversion of heart and a turning back to God. As we read when the prophet Samuel was sent to Jesse to anoint David as king, 'God looks at the heart' (1 Samuel 16:7).

Matthew's description of John in verse 3 places him first of all as the one prophesied by Isaiah 40:3. Unlike in Luke's telling of the Gospel, where John first appears in Elizabeth's womb, Matthew portrays John as an established prophet, the last of the old order of prophets who prepared God's people for the coming Messiah and the new kingdom.

By describing the way John is dressed (v. 4), Matthew links him also with Elijah, one of the most revered of the prophets, who appeared at Jesus' transfiguration, representing the whole prophetic tradition (Matthew 17:3). Matthew's audience would have been familiar with Elijah's appearance as recorded in 2 Kings 1:8. So, by quoting Isaiah's prophecy and including a physical description reminiscent of Elijah, Matthew sets John apart within the prophetic tradition as one to be listened to.

The rest of the text warns against the dangers of outward observance without inner conversion, as demonstrated by the Pharisees and Sadducees (v. 7). The Pharisees were religious purists who strictly observed the letter of the law and the oral tradition that had grown up around it. The Sadducees, a more politically motivated group, believed that only the five books of the Torah were the authentic word of God. Both groups came into conflict with Jesus through the course of his life and ministry. John calls us to prepare our hearts to be filled with the Spirit of Christ.

5 Mary and Joseph make a home

Matthew 1:18–25

We hear little of the relationship between Mary and Joseph, and what we do read is found in the few stories of Jesus' birth and childhood. Matthew's Gospel mentions Joseph most often, with ten references to him by name. Here, very early on in Matthew, we see a betrothed couple facing difficulties. Such was the culture of the time that a betrothed man was already referred to as the woman's 'husband', so breaking off an engagement was not a simple private matter. Divorce in this setting generally required a public repudiation of the wife, but Joseph is disinclined to do this (v. 19), out of a desire to care for Mary. Matthew suggests that there is genuine affection from Joseph towards Mary.

There are perhaps two possible reasons for Joseph's desire to divorce her. Maybe he doesn't believe Mary's claim that her pregnancy is the result of the action of the Holy Spirit and assumes she has had intercourse with another man; in today's setting, this would be the more likely scenario. However, an alternative view is that Joseph chooses to divorce Mary to protect the sanctity of her pregnancy, so that none would doubt the origin of the child's conception. The angel who appears in a dream then convinces him that it is God's will that Mary should become his wife.

The appearance of the angel in a dream to Joseph, the first of two such instances in Matthew's Gospel (see 2:13), links back to occasions in the Old Testament when God made his intentions known in dreams (for example, Genesis 31:10–13; 41:1–7; Daniel 7).

Convinced by the vision in his dream, Joseph marries Mary and makes a home for their son, who is to be named Jesus, meaning 'God saves'. As the angels of the Lord says in verse 21, he is 'the one who is to save his people from their sins'. A further name, 'Immanuel', meaning 'God is with us', proclaims the incarnation of God, as does John 1:14: 'The Word became flesh and lived among us'. Both Matthew and John show us an intimate God. Not only is the kingdom close at hand, but so is God.

6 Paul reminds us of our calling

Romans 1:1–7

The final character in our Advent scriptures for this week is the apostle Paul, and we focus on his opening address in the letter to the Romans. Paul adopts the conventional letter-writing style of the time with this introductory paragraph. It includes the name of the sender, the name of the receiver, and general good wishes followed by prayer and thanksgiving. Paul, however, liberally colours all these things with an overt and specific Christian emphasis, as well as a hint of what is to come in the rest of his letter.

In Paul's opening words, he draws together some of the themes and people we have considered over these last few days. He connects Jesus with the earthly line of kings through David (v. 3), and presents him as the incarnate Son of God through the Holy Spirit (v. 4). The call he gives is clear and specific: we belong to Christ, as his holy people.

Verse 1 states that Paul is 'called to be an apostle'. In simple terms, this means an envoy or ambassador, someone with authority who conveys a message from one party to another. However, it also means one who is chosen by Christ to be his disciple and a witness to his actions and words. In verses 6 and 7, Paul speaks of two other callings for his readers—first, to belong to Jesus Christ, and second, to be saints. In his understanding, these are not future events, yet to take place, but current states of being. Our calling to be saints and apostles, and to belong to Jesus Christ, is something that already sets us apart, and so we live accordingly.

Our saintly calling reminds us of our holiness: to be a saint is to be consecrated for the Lord. It reminds us of our origin—that from the beginning, humans were made in the image and likeness of God (Genesis 1:27), and that God knit each one of us together in our mother's womb (Psalm 139:13).

Surely Advent, with its focus on the incarnation and the return of Christ in glory, has the potential to focus our attention sharply on how we may reflect the nature of God, and on the need to be ever more holy and sanctified to claim our belonging to Christ.

Guidelines

Here are some questions to ponder as we think back over the week's readings.

- How can you keep focused on the Advent practice of preparation when the world around us tells us that the time to celebrate is now?
- What are some useful ways to prepare yourself for your heavenly homeland?
- How can you learn to judge others by the heart and not by outward appearance?
- What do you need to repent of and how will you act as a result?
- In what ways do you experience closeness to God?
- What is your mission, and have you chosen to accept it fully, obediently and unconditionally?
- How can you helpfully develop an Advent mindset?

The Word became flesh: John 1:1–18

This week's readings are a close study of the first 18 verses of John's Gospel. These are traditionally read at Midnight Mass on Christmas Eve, forming a rich theological meditation on Jesus' birth. For this week, we have put on one side *Guidelines*' normal practice of reading a good chunk of scripture each day. We are slowing down, with just a few verses to ponder. These opening verses of John are particularly rich, repaying the extra time spent.

John's Gospel is different from the others, and this is never more obvious than at Christmas. Where are Mary and Joseph? Bethlehem? The star? Herod? The wise men? John's different perspective can be grasped by reference to the book of Revelation, which in all likelihood emerged from the same author. In Revelation 1—3 we are introduced to a human author writing earthly letters to real places. Then, at 4:1–2, a door is opened in heaven and the writer is 'taken up', so that much of the rest of the book contains the 'heavenly perspective' on earthly situations. So too in John 1. Luke and Matthew tell us the 'earthly story'; John gives us the 'heavenly perspective'—what is really going on.

Not everything is different, though. Mark, Matthew and Luke all in their different ways tell us 'the truth' in their opening verses. Mark 1:1, for example, reads, 'The good news of Jesus Christ the Son of God' with no spoiler alert. John similarly starts by stating boldly, 'The Word was God... the Word became flesh... We have seen his glory... The one and only Son... made the Father known.' The Gospels do not gradually reveal who Jesus is—perhaps not surprisingly, since almost all the original hearers of the Gospels would already have been Jesus' disciples. Rather, they depict for us the struggle that humans experience in grasping this truth and its meaning. Thus, these opening verses of John, often called 'the prologue', repay our study, for we too know the basics. We know about Bethlehem, the shepherds and Mary, yet many of us are only just scratching the surface of what Jesus' birth really means.

Quotations are taken from my own translation of the Greek, but the notes can be used with any English Bible.

1 Beginning

'In the beginning' is not just a good way to start a story. It repeats the first two words of the Greek translation of the book of Genesis. In fact, John writes simply, 'In beginning', which is slightly awkward in Greek (as in English) but matches Genesis 1:1 precisely. The connection is deliberate. We are being taken back to before creation; that is when the story of Jesus starts.

In Genesis, God creates by speaking. We often do the same: leadership in a family, a sports team, a group of friends or a business is often about speaking out how things should be, what the goal is, how we should act in a situation. Speaking creates something new.

We are not the same as our words, yet they have an intimate connection with us. They emerge from us; they represent us; they convey who we are; they are our vehicle for engaging with others. The Old Testament draws on this idea, perhaps most notably in Isaiah 55:11. God's word is a way of speaking of God's activity in the world, without challenging the great Jewish doctrine of monotheism (Deuteronomy 6:4). God's word is clearly not separate from or competing with God himself, yet the idea of God's word being active helps bridge the gap between the transcendent, unapproachable God and our experience. In the beginning, God spoke a word and creation happened; now we see God's word continuing to interact with that creation.

There is a little more going on here, though, for these verses, particularly verse 3, move us from God's action through speaking multiple words to the idea of God's word as a single 'thing'. We should probably see this as drawing on the incorporation of Greek ideas into Jewish thought, with 'word' having the connotation of 'plan' or 'overarching logic'. God's activity in creation is not 'lots of words' but a single plan or purpose which contains everything. We are about to hear about 'the big picture', 'the theory of everything', not a little piece of the jigsaw.

Humans search for meaning and purpose. That has driven scientific understanding since the earliest days—the sense that what happens around us does so for a reason, if we can only work out the patterns and connections. The next verses will show that we have a connection with this 'word'. What you do today is not irrelevant: our story can be part of this 'big picture' of God's purpose.

2 Light

John 1:4–9

Light and darkness is perhaps the most primeval and deeply rooted metaphor in religious language. Each day, most of us experience the day as the medium in which we function: our bodies come alive, our sight works, it's relatively warm. Night is not our world. Of course, in the developed world, light and heat are at the touch of a button, so we can turn night into day, but that only re-emphasises the fact that humans are creatures of the light.

Verse 4 could be paraphrased as 'He is the life giver and the life sustainer'. Humanity needs to be not just created—with life breathed into it—but sustained (Psalm 104:27–30). It is not self-evident that life giving and life sustaining come from the same source. Many philosophies and strands of religious thinking separate the two, as if the world is left to 'get on with it' after creation, or they picture a spirit helping us to make sense of a world which is alien or even hostile. No, says John, the word that created is also the light that sustains and guides the creation.

There is conflict, though. Darkness threatens. This seems to point back to Genesis again, where God 'carved out' the habitable world from something darker (Genesis 1:1, 6; see also Psalm 104:5–9; 74:12–17). This fits our experience of any light source at night: the darkness seems infinite, the light dwarfed by it yet keeping it at bay. The end of verse 5 could be translated, 'The darkness has not overcome it' or '… understood it' (or, perhaps, 'has not mastered it'). 'Understood' rather gives 'darkness' an existence as a thinking 'power', setting light and darkness up as opposing entities, which probably gives the wrong flavour. Darkness is the threatening chaos, the reduction to dust and nothingness. It seeks not to understand but to consume.

Within that conflict, humans have their role. We are all called to be like John—witnesses, pointers, supports of the light. But something new is happening in these verses (compare Hebrews 1:1–3). The 'true' light is *entering into* the world (v. 9). This is something more than the light *shining on to* the world, as it has done since creation. Do we think of God just shining on to or truly entering into our life today? Do we just shine on to or enter into the lives and darknesses of those around us?

3 Children of God

The poetry makes clear that the failure to recognise and receive was, in effect, a rejection, a rebellion (vv. 10–11). Because the world was made through him, it ought to have recognised him. His own ought to have received him. The sense of a culpable lack of recognition of God is common in Jewish critiques of Gentiles (Romans 1:19–25), and this is perhaps the sense of verse 10: people in general have failed to recognise God, despite the fact that he is visible in his creation. Verse 11 pushes it further, with 'his own' pointing to the Jewish people. They might, in particular, have been expected to receive him, but didn't. The whole of creation has turned its back on the Creator, recapping in a sense the 'fall' in Genesis 3 and echoing Romans 3:19.

All, though, is not lost. The idea of being 'God's children' is a powerful one, used, for example, by Jesus in Matthew 5:9. Its use in verse 12 makes clear that it doesn't simply refer to all people. All are made in God's image and have God's life breathed into them, but being God's child here clearly refers to some and not all.

How do we become a child of God? Positively, it is through 'receiving' the Word, which seems to be the same as 'believing in his name'. This echoes the parable of the sower, with its focus on hearing and receiving 'the word' (Mark 4:20). Throughout the rest of John's Gospel, 'believing' is the key term describing the correct response to Jesus (John 2:11; 3:16; 6:47; 20:31). It's a useful corrective to an assumption that 'belief' means 'intellectual assent'. Belief is about accepting, receiving and welcoming.

The order of the words in verses 12 and 13 emphasises the negatives—'not… not… not'. The triplet is literally 'blood', 'will of flesh' and 'will of husband' (or 'will of man' [male]). Taken together, this points to physical conception and birth, contrasting it with a purer 'spiritual' birth. A similar contrast is explained to Nicodemus (John 3:3–8), and Jesus' clash with some Jewish people culminates in an argument over whether they are 'really' God's children (John 8:31–47). Physical descent is not enough.

For most of us, this is good news. If being 'God's child' were a matter of our parentage, we would be excluded. Instead, all we need to do is to recognise and accept God.

4 The Word made flesh

The in-carn-ation or 'en-fleshing' of the word is the distinctive, even shocking, heart of Christianity. The idea of God speaking to or appearing in our world is common across religions, but God becoming flesh is different, just as the light 'entering into' is different from the light 'shining on to' the world.

I like to tease theological students by asking whether we should talk about 'Jesus' before his incarnation. John does not: before, he speaks of 'the word', it is only afterwards that he speaks of Jesus (1:17, 29). The second person of the Trinity is certainly eternal ('the Word' was present before creation, v. 1), but if we too easily talk of Jesus before the incarnation, we fall into the idea that he 'came down'. The Word did not just 'come down'; it / he was 'enfleshed'.

John often gives 'flesh' a negative connotation (for example, 'The spirit gives life; the flesh counts for nothing', 6:63). Yet the 'Word'—God's activity in the world and his plan and purpose—became part of the mixed-up, hard, messy creation itself. Paul would describe this as an emptying or becoming poor (Philippians 2:7; 2 Corinthians 8:9). It is so striking that, as soon as John mentions this flesh, he has to remind us again that Jesus had 'glory', a divine quality (Exodus 24:16, Ezekiel 1:28) appropriate for God's 'only son'.

'The Word… lived among us, and we have seen…'. Rightly, we understand 'among us' as 'among humanity', but John really did mean that he and those around him had seen it with their own eyes (1 John 1:1–3; John 19:35). 'The word', which is God (v. 1) lived down our street; we knew him. This seems so bizarre that we may want to soften it. The sense of distance between us and God is deeply entrenched in human thought. But God has crossed that divide and joined us, entering into his creation rather than standing outside. Nothing honours my children more than if I join in their games, not watching from the outside. Being alongside someone who is suffering counts far more than words or trying to solve their problem for them. Different, overlapping, conclusions can be drawn from this: God does not keep separate or stay 'clean'; 'the flesh' is not bad—the physical aspects of life are to be embraced and celebrated; and we too need to 'enter in', not 'shine on'.

5 Grace

John's testimony prefigures Jesus' own words: 'before Abraham was, I am' (John 8:58). They point to a key aspect of the truth being asserted in these verses—that Jesus was 'more than a prophet'. His revelation of God was in a different category. Jesus / God's Word existed *before*, and then entered into our world. While verse 14 emphasises the 'flesh', verse 15 ensures that we do not make him just a 'spirit-filled prophet or teacher'.

'Fullness' (v. 16) is a difficult word to translate. It is used by Paul in Colossians 1:19: 'In [Jesus] all the fullness was pleased to dwell' (also Colossians 2:9; Ephesians 1:23). It is a term used in some Greek religious thinking of the time as a way of speaking of 'Deity', 'the Supreme Power', 'the World Soul'. At a simpler level, it could be translated as 'completeness'. The sense here perhaps is that 'he is / has everything and has shared it with us'.

The end of verse 16 is also complex. It might be translated literally, 'grace in place of grace', but is further complicated by verse 17, which contrasts 'law' (through Moses) with 'grace and truth' (through Jesus). At times, Christians have approached 'grace' as if it were only a 'New Testament' concept, as opposed to Old Testament law. This is to misread the Old Testament, though, for repeatedly it speaks of God's choice of Israel being purely a matter of grace (Deuteronomy 7:6–9; Genesis 12:1–3, used as an example of grace in Romans 4). It would also be theologically difficult to suggest that God suddenly changed the way he relates to humanity. If so, might he not do it again? Maybe he did so 600 years after Jesus, and we are getting it wrong now?

No; God always worked through grace. The grace found in Jesus is 'grace in place of grace'. However, something has changed. Rather than 'grace expressed through law' we have 'unadulterated pure grace'. God's grace received through a middle-man (for example, Moses) has a lower quality than grace received directly from God's fullness.

'Truth' is important throughout John's Gospel: we should worship in 'spirit and truth' (John 4:24). Jesus' words are true (John 8:14, 16), often with the sense of 'real', 'reliable' or 'substantial' rather than partial or limited. God has always worked through his undeserved kindness and mercy (grace), and that has become fully visible, accessible and 'made real' in Jesus.

6 The Son makes the Father known

Here the introduction finishes, for in verse 19 we swoop back down from this 'heavenly perspective' to the historical circumstances of John the Baptist's ministry. And what is the climax? It is not that the Word became flesh and entered into his world. That is earth-shattering, turning religion, philosophy and our understanding of humanity on their heads, but it is not what matters most. The climax is that Jesus 'makes God known'.

The incarnation itself, it seems, is a mechanism. Its purpose was to achieve something else. It was the way truly to make God known. From 'outside', God could only 'shine into' the world; he could only speak through prophets and laws. But, it seems, that is not sufficient. If God's aim is to make himself known, the only way is for him to enter into our world, to share our lives, to be alongside us as one of us.

Ignorance of God, therefore, seems to be the biggest problem—indeed, not just ignorance but the sense that God is unknowable or unreachable. 'No one has ever seen God.' The Old Testament suggests that this is because of God's glory: to see him would be to die (Isaiah 6:5; Exodus 33:20). Most people today would share the sense that God, by definition, can't be seen. The old hymn describes him as 'immortal, invisible, God only wise, in light inaccessible hid from our eyes'.

The problem, though, has been solved. Jesus, 'who is God himself', has made him known. In the words of Paul in 2 Corinthians 4:6, 'For the God who said, "Let light shine out of darkness" is the one who shone in our hearts, giving the light of the knowledge of the glory of God in the face of Jesus Christ.' John 1:18 links us back to verse 1: they both try to express the idea that Jesus is God ('the Word was God'; 'God the only son') while distinguishing him from God. Who could possibly reveal God accurately? Only God himself. There can be no mediator.

This is an important reminder. We cannot be mediators. We cannot reveal God to people; if we could, he would have simply sent prophets to make him known (Hebrews 1:1–2). We can point people to Jesus (1:36, 45), but, in the words of Archbishop Sentamu, 'Our job is to lead people to Jesus and leave them there.' The only reliable way of seeing God is to look at Jesus.

Guidelines

- God entered into our life; how might we enter into God's?
- God did not just shine on to the mess of our world; he cared enough to enter into it. How might we 'enter into' the difficulties borne by other people?
- God brought light into our world. Where in your life does it feel as if the darkness threatens to overwhelm the light?
- How can you point to the light? Whom might you point to the light? Are you tempted to set yourself up as the light—as the one who reveals God?
- Celebrate the fact that you are God's child. Drink deeply of God's grace.

FURTHER READING

R. Bauckham, *Gospel of Glory: Major themes in Johannine theology*, Baker Academic, 2015.

J. Duff and J. Collicutt McGrath, *Meeting Jesus: Human responses to a yearning God*, SPCK, 2006.

J.R. Michaels, *The Gospel of John*, Eerdmans, 2010.

N.T. Wright, *John for Everyone*, Westminister, 2004.

Great Christmas words: Luke 2:8–20

'God contracted to a span' was the way Charles Wesley described the incarnation in his hymn 'Let earth and heaven combine'. It is hard for us to imagine things that are profoundly 'contracted' or concentrated. Scientists tell us that all the matter of the universe was very, very small the split-second before the 'big bang' occurred. And here we are, living on a tiny fragment of the universe, called earth. We can feel and enjoy on our faces the wisp of a breeze, which weighs almost nothing, or hear the magic of a moving piece of music, the sound of which can hardly be weighed! Such things are so 'diluted' compared with the matter before the explosion, but they are still profound.

In Luke 2:8–20 we hear of the birth of Jesus. The telling of it requires the involvement of heaven and earth—angelic choir and rough shepherds—but it also concentrates many significant and profound biblical words and phrases. During this week of our Christmas celebration, we will explore six of them, considering some of the background and implications of these words. By doing so, we will be better able to appreciate the 'contraction of God into a span'. We will also read a psalm each day, one that echoes something of the word or phrase under consideration.

There will still be many other features of this concentrated text that we will simply have to note and leave. For instance, there is the phrase, 'an angel of the Lord appeared', which evokes many other stories, such as Gideon's call (Judges 6:11–12). Then, what about the command or encouragement, 'Do not be afraid' (v. 10; see Matthew 14:27; 28:10; Mark 5:36)? We do not have time to delve into the profound meaning and implications of the God-given 'signs' (v. 12) that are so important in John's Gospel as it seeks to unravel the deep mystery of the incarnation and birth of Jesus.

For now, though, we seek the breeze on our faces and the divine music for our hearts.

1 Good news

Psalm 40:1–5, 9–17; Luke 2:8–11

Picture the scene: half-conscious shepherds are huddled together for warmth, maybe complaining of the cold or the silliness of sheep, when suddenly they are startled out of their minds by the blazing appearance of an angel. They are highlighted by the glory of God, like rabbits in a headlight. This must be the end for them!

Yet the message is 'I am bringing you good news…' William Barclay comments on the word for 'good news', 'When we come to study it we are of necessity at the very heart and centre of the Christian faith' (*New Testament Words*, p. 101). But the shepherds, frightened to death, do not know this yet.

Perhaps, however, they would recall the Psalms, where the 'good news' is all about God's deliverance, faithfulness and steadfast love. God delivers the psalmist from evil—from those who 'seek to snatch away my life' (v. 14)—and from his own iniquity (v. 12). Perhaps, too, the words of Isaiah 52:7 would reverberate in their minds: 'How beautiful… are the feet of the messenger who announces peace… who says to Zion, "Your God reigns."'

Both the personal and the corporate dimensions have the same core. Good news is about God acting decisively and publicly to establish his righteous, loving rule; to deliver us from those who oppress and humiliate, and to restore well-being.

Originally, in Greek, the word 'good news' meant the reward given to the messenger bringing the news (see 2 Samuel 4:10). Only later, it began to mean, as here, the message itself. But paramount for us is that the good news is about God acting to deliver individuals and his people. It is 'the return of the Lord to Zion' (Isaiah 52:8).

So how is God coming to Zion? According to this angel, he comes in the birth of a child in Bethlehem. Our minds might quickly move to all the other fascinating New Testament connections with the 'good news' or 'gospel' (for instance, the gospel of truth, Galatians 2:5; of hope, Colossians 1:23; of peace, Ephesians 6:15; of the crucified and risen Christ, 1 Corinthians 15:1–11). However, the shepherds would grasp this central truth from their knowledge of the Old Testament. To them, it would mean that God was coming to deliver. This baby is 'a Saviour, who is the Messiah, the Lord' (v. 11).

2 Great joy

Psalm 96; Luke 2:10

How are we to understand the phrase 'good news of great joy'? Is joy the content of the good news? Is it all about joy, how we can get it and what it is? I think not. Joy is the outcome of, or response to, the reality that is the substance of the good news. The content of the good news is God and his deliverance, but, as a result of God's loving intervention, people will experience joy.

'Let the heavens be glad, and let the earth rejoice... Then shall all the trees of the forest sing for joy before the Lord; for he is coming' (Psalm 96:11–13). Why? Because God is going to deliver them from their captivity and oppression.

Joy is something that we may experience and express on many occasions: when we have gathered the harvest in successfully, when we are celebrating the gift of love and new beginnings at a wedding feast, when a child has been born into our family and so there is a sense of achievement and well-being for the future. All of these events generate within us that powerful sense of joy—rich happiness mixed with gratitude; satisfaction bubbling out as laughter. But 'great joy' must be reserved for something even more fulfilling, even more ground-breaking, even more satisfying. In Luke 2:10, it is focused on or fuelled by the birth of a child. But why should the birth of someone else's child—not in their own family, neighbourhood or even city—be the source of such deep joy?

We see 'great joy' when, at a cup final, a team scores the winning goal. We see it in the players as they dash towards the crowd and throw themselves over each other. We see it in the exuberance, mixed with relief, of their responding supporters. We see it in the thronging multitudes as they greet the returning heroes making their way home through the city in an open-topped bus. Their joy is multiplied by the long journey to get to the final, and by the intensity of the cup final match itself. Every twist and turn of the match adds to the joy at the victory. So here in Luke, it has been centuries in the making but now the victory is secure. The tension of waiting, the years of desperation, are all washed away: a Saviour has been born.

3 A saviour

Shepherds they were and probably always would be—shepherds in the city of David. David: now there was a shepherd if ever there was one! But he got away and became king. Did shepherds tell each other the stories of his life? He had certainly been Israel's Saviour, hadn't he? The people of God had been humiliated, trapped and hemmed in by the Philistine menace. Most of all, they'd been terrified by the monster Goliath: 'The Philistine said, "Today I defy the ranks of Israel! Give me a man, that we may fight together." When Saul and all Israel heard these words... they were dismayed and greatly afraid' (1 Samuel 17:10–11).

'But it was one of us that did him in!' the shepherds would boast together. 'Never mind the shining armour and great shields of the soldiers; it was one of us, with a sling, that did for him. Stone dead!' They laughed together at the joke.

Yes, the shepherds understood about a saviour. David's courage against and defeat of Goliath meant that the Israelite warriors became free to live without the constant threat of death, free to return to their families and raise their crops, free to trade and travel.

A saviour risked his life to set all the rest free from everything that diminished human flourishing. This saviour went on to lead his followers to maintain that freedom, and was eventually appointed king of God's people.

'Saving' is a great theme of Luke's Gospel. We can glean something of its breadth from earlier references, in chapter 1. Mary 'rejoices in God my Saviour' when she receives Elizabeth's blessing (1:39–55). Perhaps he is 'God my Saviour' because he has chosen her to carry his son (vv. 48–49), in which case this 'saving' would mean that she had been lifted out of her mundane existence as a peasant girl in Nazareth to become the intimate and honoured partner of God, or because this son would reverse the status quo (vv. 51–54). Then, Zechariah's prophecy speaks about a mighty saviour who will redeem Israel and deliver the nation from its enemies (vv. 69–71). But he has in his sights far more than just external enemies, like the Roman Empire. This salvation will encompass 'the forgiveness of their sins' and light for those overwhelmed by the shadow of death, and will eventually 'guide our feet into the way of peace' (vv. 77–79).

4 Peace

Hardly have the shepherds grasped the message of the angel (let alone its meaning) when their visual and auditory sensory mechanisms, already severely challenged, are truly overwhelmed by a multitude of angels—the heavenly host, the divine army.

When Isaiah encountered these terrifying beings, he was left severely shaken, as was the very fabric of the temple: 'The pivots on the thresholds shook at the voices of those who called' (Isaiah 6:4).

What verdict will they pronounce to the shepherds? What judgement have they come to enact?

'Glory to God in the highest heaven, and on earth peace among those whom he favours' (Luke 2:14). They bring a message of peace! As we read in Isaiah, 'How beautiful upon the mountains are the feet of the messenger who announces peace' (52:7).

This peace means that God is on the move, that Israel has been pardoned of all her sins, that he is going to comfort his people. He will protect them, defeat their enemies and, as in the exodus march through the wilderness, go in front of them and behind. God will create a 'safe space' for his people once again—a place where they can thrive without fear of oppression, disturbance and violent upheaval.

The child announced by the angels, whom the shepherds will soon see, will bring peace to the blind, restoring their sight; peace to the rejected, affirming them as loved by God; peace to those oppressed by evil spirits, setting them free; peace to the bereaved, restoring their dead to life; peace to the wild sea, calming it. Peace involves the end of conflict, the undoing of destruction, the righting of wrongs, the restoration of conditions for the flourishing of life and the establishment of the rule of God. And one day, after all his struggles with evil, ending in his violent and brutal death under the combined Roman and Jewish authorities, he will stand in front of his disciples and say, 'Peace be with you' (Luke 24:36).

In response to the plea of the psalmist, 'Restore us again, O God of our salvation' (85:4), comes the promise that God 'will speak peace to his people' (v. 8). 'Surely his salvation is at hand for those who fear him, that his glory may dwell in our land' (v. 9).

5 Shepherds

This great passage from Luke's Gospel begins and ends with shepherds: 'There were shepherds living in the fields… The shepherds returned…' (vv. 8, 20). They are also pivotal for the drama of this passage. It is their decision that enables the Christmas story and, ultimately, the gospel story to unfold. 'The shepherds said to one another, "Let us go now to Bethlehem and see this thing that has taken place…"' (v. 15). How different it would have been if they had said, 'We've been dreaming!' or 'Come on, guys, remember our duty—no time off for us!'

We also need to note that their inclusion in the invitation to see Jesus and be transformed is itself 'gospel'. Shepherds were considered unclean. They lived in the fields, so they couldn't carry out the necessary washing rituals before worship. They were constantly involved with unclean things, including contact with sick animals, and blood at every birth. That is one reason why 'shepherds' is a great gospel word: the birth of Jesus rescued them!

Another reason concerns the history of the word. In Ezekiel 34, God casti-gates Israel's leaders for not looking after his people properly. Many poten-tates in the ancient world described themselves as 'shepherds', but God says, in effect, 'If you want the glory, take the responsibility.' Even further back, Moses was a shepherd before God called him to lead his people. David too was a shepherd and learnt skills in that role which enabled him to kill Goliath and 'catapult' himself towards his own kingship.

Psalm 23 reminds us that God himself can well be considered a shep-herd (see also Psalms 80:1 and 95:7). Later, Jesus was to call himself 'the good shepherd' (John 10:11–16), thus making the word extremely valuable within Christian vocabulary. Peter described himself and other elders in terms of shepherding language: 'I exhort the elders among you to tend the flock of God' (1 Peter 5:1–6; see Peter's renewed call from Jesus in John 21:15–17). In this transferred sense, the word has become an honoured one within the Christian tradition: ministers are 'pastors', meaning 'shepherds', with Jesus himself as 'the chief shepherd' (1 Peter 5:4).

Christmas would hardly be Christmas without the shepherds—not only in our nativity presentations and carols, but also in the reality of the gospel. In inviting them to the manger, God was demonstrating the heart of the gospel for ordinary, even despised, people, who have a special place within his redemptive love.

6 Glory and praise

Psalm 148; Luke 2:9–14, 20

It would have been a most unusual sight—a group of shepherds making their way from Bethlehem back to the fields as the dawn broke, singing praise to God (v. 20). As we have seen, shepherds were not noted for their piety, so what brought about this paeon of praise?

First we should remember that they had experienced 'the glory of the Lord' (v. 9). When the angel first appeared, they were enveloped in the shining glory that indicated God's presence to Israel. This had happened before, at key moments such as the dedication of the temple (2 Chronicles 5:14; 7:1–4), and it would happen later at the transfiguration of Jesus (Luke 9:28–35). The sense of God's presence was awe-inspiring and almost tangible. 'Glory' indicates the reality of God made manifest to human beings—the weight of God's revelation concentrated into a dazzling experience. For the shepherds, then, it was not only the angels' message but also the divine encounter that empowered them to go to Bethlehem.

'Glory' was also the human and angelic response to encountering God. Thus the shepherds heard 'the heavenly host, praising God and saying, "Glory to God in the highest heaven"' (vv. 13–14). To see angels praising God is not as common in the Bible as we might think. Psalm 148:1–2 is a rare example; perhaps the seraphim in Isaiah's vision were praising God too as they cried, 'Holy, Holy, Holy' (Isaiah 6:3).

In glorifying God, this angelic army identified themselves as being on the 'good' side. There were enough Jewish folklore stories of the conflict between the sons of light and of darkness for it to be a daunting possibility that they were Satan's forces. More than that, they also modelled for the shepherds the proper response to God, mirrored for us again in Revelation 4:6–11.

The shepherds, however, can only fulfil their response to this encounter with God's glory and the call of God's glory once they have journeyed to Bethlehem, visited the manger and seen the baby—the fulfilment of God's word to them personally but also to his people over many generations. The full Christmas experience involves more than an experience of transcendence and a magnificent performance of Handel's *Messiah*! These great human experiences can release us and prepare us to praise God, but, to truly glorify God, the shepherds required a personal encounter with 'a Saviour, the Messiah' (v. 11). Luke is giving a model for 'all the people' (v. 10).

Guidelines

- Which of this week's six words or phrases gripped your mind or stirred your heart the most?
- Reflect on people in our society and in your circle of friends who might feel they are on the edge of God's concern, as the shepherds did. Inevitably we think of refugees and migrants driven from their homelands, separated from family and so on. But what about those who are sleeping rough, the lonely older person, those with mental illnesses, or prisoners and their families? Pray for these people over the Christmas period. Pray that God will find a way to visit them with his good news. Are there ways that you or your church family could be God's 'angels' to them?
- What can help us re-experience the wonder and deep world-changing truth of the Christmas story? Be alert to new ways in which God may bring his truth into your life.
- This 'breaking news' of a saviour came to the bewildered shepherds, but it was not a truth for them alone. They carried the burden of delivering it to all: it is 'for all the people'. Once we have been grasped by the 'good news', we too are commissioned to pass it on. How can we find ways to share the truth of Christmas? If your church is involved, how can you support it?

FURTHER READING

William Barclay, *New Testament Words*, SCM, 1964.

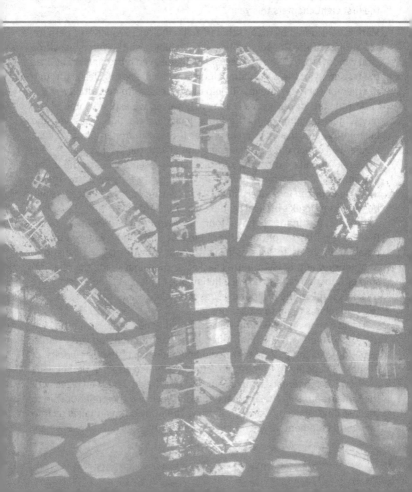

Guidelines forthcoming issue

DAVID SPRIGGS

A new year means a 'new' Gospel writer for us. A significant commitment for *Guidelines* is to engage in some depth with the lectionary Gospel. That is why we provide three weeks' notes in each issue for it. This year's Gospel is Mark and we are very fortunate to have Steve Motyer taking us through the first eight chapters this year.

Mark is considered by many scholars to be the core Gospel text, perhaps the earliest of the Gospels we have in our Bibles, so this offers us with a vital window on the story of Jesus. It is made even more significant if, as the testimony of the early church indicates, we are seeing Jesus through the memory of Peter. Steve will help us see Jesus with new vitality.

At the start of our year's readings, however, we explore some of the many 'new beginnings' in the Bible, including creation, Passover, the incarnation and the 'new creation' for those who are 'in Christ'. These studies will enrich our spiritual engagement with the 'new year'.

Derek Tidball's exposition of Colossians presents us with the vision and impact of a 'cosmic Christ'—God's adequate answer to the messy universe depicted in Genesis and in which we find ourselves. Here we will benefit from Derek's biblical scholarship and clarity of writing.

We are fortunate to have four new writers in *Guidelines*. David Beresford is Director of the Catholic Bible School and he will explore the parables of Jesus to give us insight about growth in God's kingdom. Another new author is Anthony Thacker. Anthony has made the relationship of Christian faith to science fiction one of his special interests. Here he takes some of the profound issues that science fiction uses as its subtext and relates them to biblical insights.

David Cohen and David Dewey are the other new writers and they are joined by Hugh Williamson in offering us contributions on the Psalms. Hugh looks at the psalms that begin and end each of the 'five books' of Psalms. By spotlighting these structurally situated psalms, he helps us see how we can reread them for our own day. David Dewey engages with the Hallel Psalms on the approach to Holy Week and their relationship to the last days of Jesus' earthly ministry. Then David Cohen takes us into the world of lament, as exemplified in many of the Psalms. While we are familiar with praise and thanksgiving, as well as confession, in the Psalms, lament is a stranger world—but one which is vital if our spirituality is to withstand the shocks and challenges that life brings to us all.

Our final three authors bring more riches from the Bible into our ordinary lives. Antony Billington has reflected extensively on biblical insights into our work and offers us deep and challenging perspectives on the way many of us spend 25% of our time. He helps us see our attitudes in this context as a crucial part of our spirituality. Tim Davy focuses on the theme of adoption, both the power of the metaphor in scripture (including its place in the purposes of God) and its impact on children and adults now.

As we journey from Epiphany through Lent to resurrection, it is appropriate that we have some stimulating notes on this central part of our faith. Ian Paul introduces us to some of the rich and far-reaching aspects of Christ's resurrection through the writings of Paul.

Author profile: Michael Parsons

The Bible has always been central to my Christian understanding and my walk with the Lord. It is the story into which I bring my own story, the narrative into which my personal narrative fits. It is somehow the word of God, a word that informs my thinking and forms my life. And, primarily, it is that which points me to Jesus Christ, the incarnated Word of God, in whom I have everything.

This has not always been the case, however. Born into a non-Christian family, I was only introduced to the Bible at around 15 years of age, when a close relative passed away and I was left with nowhere to turn. In grace, and quite inexplicably, I was led to start reading the Bible; beginning at Genesis, giving-up somewhere in Leviticus. It was a first attempt to grasp something (or someone) outside of myself and my very limited, concrete surroundings.

At my later conversion to Christ, I read and reread the Bible, attending services where the text was expounded and applied, and it came to life for me. I saw lives changed. This was, I discovered, a book that could speak into my context, a book that could move me, inspire me and guide me. In my university years I attended a church in which the pastor would expound doctrine, after the manner of Martyn Lloyd-Jones, and I was attracted to the Bible's teaching.

It wasn't until I fell from grace, rebelling against the Lord who had given me his word, that I came to a new realisation of the significance of that word. In the complexity of my own fallenness I reread the scripture again, seeing there a story into which I fitted. Here, in the Bible, were people who were not perfect, who did not always know what God wanted of them, who sometimes made drastic mistakes, but people who knew that in turning to the Lord they would find grace, forgiveness and new life. They recognised in their best moments that in Jesus Christ they were righteous, accepted by God. They discovered God to be their Father. I realised that the Bible was not the straightforward 'text book' I had thought, but the inspired spiritual reflection of believing people who had walked with God in good and in difficult times.

That amended my view of scripture. For some years now I've read through the Bible every twelve months or so. Beginning with the Psalms, I read the rest in a certain order, in lengthy portions, praying through the text, reflecting on the experience of God—theirs and my own—seeking to see the words as enculturated in the period of composition, but some-how, through the wonderful work of the Spirit, applied to my own time and situation. The pivot in all of this is grasping the central importance of Jesus Christ to the whole of scripture and to my own life and well-being, and, I would say, grasping the importance of experiencing God through the Spirit as he informs our thinking and forms our lives to exhibit something of Christ himself.

This has been the backbone, the foundation of my teaching of theology over the years. I've been blessed to teach at Murdoch University and Vose Seminary in Perth, Western Australia, for some years; more recently, to commission books at Paternoster and now at BRF. My passion in teaching and editing is that Jesus Christ might be glorified in who we are and what we do, and that the scripture might have a pivotal role in our spiritual formation and mission.

See page 148 for information on Michael Parsons' new book, Praying the Bible with Luther.

Recommended reading

CHRISTMAS
THROUGH THE
KEYHOLE

Luke's glimpses of Advent

DEREK TIDBALL

BRF Advent Book

BRF's 2017 Advent book leads us through December and up to Epiphany with the famous songs of Jesus' birth in Luke's Gospel, plus further songs from the New Testament. The author is the acclaimed writer and speaker **Derek Tidball**. The following extract is from the Introduction and the reading for 2 December.

In our house, Christmas is always a time for music. We rejoice in going to concerts, buying new recordings of old carols with their familiar words and tunes and equally welcome new compositions, or new collections of our favourite performers. Christmas without music is as inconceivable as Christmas without presents or turkey…

Soaked in the older scriptures of the Jewish people, the songs Luke records in his inspired Gospel—the songs of Mary, Zechariah, Simeon, and the angels at Bethlehem—reveal the wondrous depths that for us 'in the town of David, a Saviour has been born to us. He is the Messiah' (Luke 2:11). Their words are often those of the Old Testament, their style one of passionate yet reverent worship; their tone is one of humility, yet their rhythm indicates confident upbeat praise…

Let me ask a personal question. Do you like looking through keyholes? It is probably not the done thing to admit to such curiosity in polite company but the truth is many of us are pretty inquisitive… This book invites us to treat the songs of the Saviour's birth as keyholes through which we can spy amazing things. As we peep through our metaphorical keyholes, our eyes don't immediately settle on a crib or a crying infant. They lead us first to view the whole story of God's dealings with Israel that has led to the arrival of the Saviour. They lead us through pain, agony and failure, to discover the faithful mercy of God who, in sending a baby to Bethlehem, gives hope to his people and the wider world. We get to the manger, but only after negotiating our way through a longer story first…

Each day's comment is concluded with a text on which the reader is encouraged to meditate. To meditate is to fill our minds with truth from God or about God and to chew it over in our thinking. Five questions may help us to get started. What does this text mean? What does it teach about God? How far do I believe what it states? What difficulties do I have with this text and how can I overcome them? How does it apply to me today?

2 December: Daughter of grace

Read Luke 1:26–45.

Not infrequently, the songs that rise to the top of the charts today are not original creations, but fresh recordings by new artists of songs that have been around for a good time. A new voice, new arrangements, instruments, and technology, give the songs from long ago a new lease of life. Sometimes triggered by the personal experience of the new artist, they are creative re-presentations to communicate to a changing situation. So it was, in part, with Mary's song.

Mary is one of a long line of women in Israel for whom giving birth is the crucial issue. From Sarah, through Rachel and Hannah, down to cousin Elizabeth, we learn of several childless women who miraculously conceive and whose children not only bring joy to the family but go on to play a critical role in securing the future of Israel. Unlike these women, Mary is not infertile. She's a young, vulnerable teenager who is a virgin (Luke 1:27, 34). Since she has not yet married, her virginity is a virtue, not a matter of shame. No wonder that when the news that she will conceive a child is brought to her by the angel Gabriel, she's confused and 'troubled'. With apparently no one to turn to, she goes to visit her older cousin Elizabeth, who is also surprisingly pregnant, knowing that they'd at least have something in common. While she is there, she bursts into song—the song we know as the Magnificat, because it glorifies the Lord.

Was Mary's song original? Not exactly. It shows great similarities to Hannah's song after she had given birth to Samuel (1 Samuel 2:1–10). Their songs celebrate God's gracious initiative in coming to the rescue of Israel through the birth of a child. Hannah's 'prayer represents a turning point in Israel's history. It closed an age which at times bordered on anarchy, a period of shame and humiliation... [and] opened the door to Israel's greatness.' What happened under Samuel was merely a pointer to the greater achievements that would occur with the coming of Jesus.

Mary does not draw on Hannah's song alone. Line after line cascading from her lips comes from the Psalms, including Psalms 34, 35, 89 and 103. She may be young and female, and therefore probably uneducated, but she is devout. These psalms would have been sung sabbath after sabbath in the Nazareth synagogue and she has imbibed them deeply in her spirit. They have become a part of her. So, when the occasion arises, the appropriate words are all to hand, woven into a fresh new tapestry.

After the opening declaration ('My soul magnifies the Lord'), God is the subject of every sentence. The song does not boast that she is to become a mother, but rather that God, the Mighty One, is coming to the rescue, being merciful to Israel and proving faithful to his promise. We would have understood if the song expressed some angst about her sudden and unexpected condition. What will happen to her? What will people's reactions be? How will she cope? Yet the song is remarkably free from her own concerns and worries and astonishingly focused on God. God must be the starting point for all our faith. If we have a wrong view of him, we will have a distorted and probably dysfunctional faith.

When she does briefly speak of herself, she is not the subject, not centre stage. God still remains the subject. He is the giver and she is the surprising recipient of his grace. Her 'lowliness' isn't pseudo-humility but actual fact. From what we know of her, as a young teenage girl, she wasn't significant in other people's eyes. She also seems to have been relatively poor, judging by the offering that she and Joseph made in the temple (Luke 2:24). Coming from that backwater, Nazareth, she really was insignificant. She didn't merit any particular attention. Without qualification or entitlement, God chose her to be the mother of his incarnate son. She was 'blessed' indeed, as God poured his grace into her life.

What a remarkable thing for God to do, to trust the salvation of the world to a vulnerable, unwed teenage girl and, eventually, to Joseph, who was probably nothing much to be proud of either as a manual labourer from Nazareth. But that's the extraordinary thing about God. It is the way he has always worked. He didn't choose the nation of Israel for its strength or size (Deuteronomy 7:7–9) and he doesn't choose us because we're somebodies, but rather because we're nobodies (1 Corinthians 1:26–29). Mary fits the picture. She is honoured because she is the daughter of God's amazing grace.

Like Mary, we have no cause to boast in ourselves but only in the grace of God. I wonder if, like her, we're so steeped in scripture that we have the vocabulary to express the wonder of that grace.

For meditation:

'Blessed are the poor in spirit, for theirs is the kingdom of heaven' (Matthew 5:3).

To order a copy of this book, please turn to the order form on page 149.

Books from familiar authors

We have a number of books recently published or about to be published, written by authors who may be familiar to you. Whether you have a passion for prayer or pilgrimage, there's something for everyone with our wide variety of topics. Develop your understanding or learn something entirely new!

The Recovery of Joy
Finding the path from rootlessness to returning home

NAOMI STARKEY

pb, 978 0 85746 518 4 £7.99

Naomi Starkey, the previous editor of *New Daylight*, is back with another amazing title. Using a refreshing and unusual blend of story and biblical exposition, she traces a journey that begins in rootlessness and despair and takes a wanderer across the sea to a series of islands. These islands are the setting for a series of events and encounters through which the wanderer emerges from that initial rootlessness and makes a progression through healing to a rediscovery of the joy of feeling at the centre of God's loving purpose. *The Recovery of Joy* shows how we can find a path back to connection with God, the source of joy, even from the bleakest points of life.

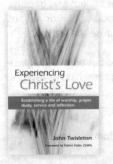

Experiencing Christ's Love
Establishing a life of worship, prayer, study, service and reflection

JOHN TWISLETON

pb, 978 0 85746 517 7 £7.99

In this new title, John Twisleton, a familiar BRF author, reminds us of Jesus' gracious challenge to love God with heart, soul and mind, and to love our neighbour as ourselves. Against the backdrop of the message of God's unconditional love in Jesus Christ, he delivers a wake-up call to the basic Christian patterns of worship, prayer, study, service and reflection. These, he claims, serve to take God's hand in ours, leading us into his divine possibilities.

Pilgrim Journeys
Pilgrimage for walkers and armchair travellers

SALLY WELCH
pb, 978 0 85746 513 9 £8.99

The current editor of *New Daylight*, Sally Welch, has written this guide to pilgrimage, for those who wish to make a physical journey and for so-called 'armchair travellers'. The book explores the less travelled pilgrim routes of the UK and beyond.

Each chapter explores a different aspect of pilgrimage, offering reflections and indicating some of the spiritual lessons to be learned from pilgrimage, that may be practised at home. This absorbing book shows how insights gained on the journey can be incorporated into everyday life, bringing new ways of relationship with God and with our fellow Christians, offering support and encouragement as we face life's joys and challenges.

Facing Death

RACHEL BOULDING
978 0 85746 564 1 £3.99

Rachel Boulding's notes from the May 2016 issue of *New Daylight* have been expanded and made available in our 'Bible readings for special times' series, by popular demand. Many readers found Rachel's honest and insightful thoughts about facing her own diagnosis touching and inspiring. With moving vulnerability and without denying the difficult reality of the situation, Rachel suggests a way to confront terminal illness with faith and hope in a loving God.

500th anniversary of the Lutheran Reformation

Praying the Bible with Luther
A simple approach to everyday prayer

MICHAEL PARSONS
978 0 85746 503 0 £8.99

Michael Parsons, one of BRF's commissioning editors, has written this book exploring how to pray through the Bible in the same way that Luther did. With the 500th anniversary of the Lutheran Reformation taking place this year, this book is ideally placed not only to give information about who Luther was but also to suggest a new way of praying and engaging with the Bible.

Beginning each time of prayer with a Bible passage, Luther would meditate on it with four 'strands' in mind: teaching, thanksgiving, repentance and supplication. Then he would pray, having his thoughts shaped by his reading, praying God's words after him, confident of God's grace. *Praying the Bible with Luther* explains this method, demonstrates it and encourages readers to follow Luther's example, helping us to turn scripture into prayer and to pray it into our own lives today.

This is more than a simple approach to everyday prayer, it's a deep book for those who desire to be serious about prayer. Highly commended for use personally and with small groups.

DAVID COFFEY OBE, GLOBAL AMBASSADOR, BMS WORLD MISSION

To order a copy of any of the books featured above, please use the order form on page 149. BRF books are also available from your local Christian bookshop or from **brfonline.org.uk**

To order

Online: brfonline.org.uk
Telephone: +44 (0)1865 319700
Mon–Fri 9.15–17.30

Delivery times within the UK are normally
15 working days. Prices are correct at the time of
going to press but may change without prior notice.

Title	Price	Qty	Total
Christmas through the Keyhole	£6.99		
Recovery of Joy	£7.99		
Experiencing Christ's Love	£7.99		
Pilgrim Journeys	£8.99		
Facing Death	£3.99		
Praying the Bible with Luther	£8.99		

POSTAGE AND PACKING CHARGES			
Order value	UK	Europe	Rest of world
Under £7.00	£1.25	£3.00	£5.50
£7.00–£29.99	£2.25	£5.50	£10.00
£30.00 and over	FREE	Prices on request	

Total value of books	
Postage and packing	
Total for this order	

Please complete in BLOCK CAPITALS

Title .... First name/initials .... Surname...

Address...

....Postcode.........................

Acc. No. .... Telephone ....

Email..

Please keep me informed about BRF's books and resources ❑ by email ❑ by post
Please keep me informed about the wider work of BRF ❑ by email ❑ by post

Method of payment

❑ Cheque (made payable to BRF) ❑ MasterCard / Visa

Card no. ☐☐☐☐ ☐☐☐☐ ☐☐☐☐ ☐☐☐☐ ☐☐☐☐ ☐☐☐☐

Valid from M M Y Y Expires M M Y Y Security code* ☐☐☐
Last 3 digits on the reverse of the card

Signature* .... Date .... /.......... /..........
*ESSENTIAL IN ORDER TO PROCESS YOUR ORDER

Please return this form to: BRF, 15 The Chambers, Vineyard, Abingdon OX14 3FE | enquiries@brf.org.uk
To read our terms and find out about cancelling your order, please visit **brfonline.org.uk/terms**.

The Bible Reading Fellowship (BRF) is a Registered Charity (233280)

How to encourage Bible reading in your church

BRF has been helping individuals connect with the Bible for over 90 years. We want to support churches as they seek to encourage church members into regular Bible reading.

Order a Bible reading resources pack

This pack is designed to give your church the tools to publicise our Bible reading notes. It includes:

- Sample Bible reading notes for your congregation to try.
- Publicity resources, including a poster.
- A church magazine feature about Bible reading notes.

The pack is free, but we welcome a £5 donation to cover the cost of postage. If you require a pack to be sent outside the UK or require a specific number of sample Bible reading notes, please contact us for postage costs. More information about what the current pack contains is available on our website.

How to order and find out more

- Visit **biblereadingnotes.org.uk/for-churches**
- Telephone BRF on +44 (0)1865 319700 Mon–Fri 9.15–17.30
- Write to us at BRF, 15 The Chambers, Vineyard, Abingdon OX14 3FE

Keep informed about our latest initiatives

We are continuing to develop resources to help churches encourage people into regular Bible reading, wherever they are on their journey. Join our email list at **biblereadingnotes.org.uk/helpingchurches** to stay informed about the latest initiatives that your church could benefit from.

Introduce a friend to our notes

We can send information about our notes and current prices for you to pass on. Please contact us.

Transforming Lives and Communities

BRF is a charity that is passionate about making a difference through the Christian faith. We want to see lives and communities transformed through our creative programmes and resources for individuals, churches and schools. We are doing this by resourcing:

- **Christian growth and understanding of the Bible.** Through our Bible reading notes, books, digital resources, Quiet Days and other events, we're resourcing individuals, groups and leaders in churches for their own spiritual journey and for their ministry.

- **Church outreach in the local community.** BRF is the home of three programmes that churches are embracing to great effect as they seek to engage with their local communities: Messy Church, Who Let The Dads Out? and The Gift of Years.

- **Teaching Christianity in primary schools.** Our Barnabas in Schools team is working with primary-aged children and their teachers, enabling them to explore Christianity creatively within the school curriculum.

- **Children's and family ministry.** Through our Barnabas in Churches and Faith in Homes websites and published resources, we're working with churches and families, enabling children under 11, and the adults working with them, to explore Christianity creatively and bring the Bible alive.

Do you share our vision?

Sales of our books and Bible reading notes cover the cost of producing them. However, our other programmes are funded primarily by donations, grants and legacies. If you share our vision, would you help us to transform even more lives and communities? Your prayers and financial support are vital for the work that we do.

- You could support BRF's ministry with a one-off gift or regular donation (using the response form on page 153).
- You could consider making a bequest to BRF in your will (page 152).
- You could encourage your church to support BRF as part of your church's giving to home mission—perhaps focusing on a specific area of our ministry, or a particular member of our Barnabas team.
- Most important of all, you could support BRF with your prayers.

Make a lasting difference through a gift in your will

What do we want our children to care about as they grow and take their place in society? It's a big issue and one that The Bible Reading Fellowship (BRF) cares about deeply.

One of the ways in which we seek to address this issue is by teaching Christianity in primary schools. Our Barnabas in Schools team works with primary-aged children and their teachers, enabling them to explore Christianity creatively and confidently within the school curriculum. 33,000 children experience our Barnabas RE Days each year.

The schools team recently introduced two special Barnabas RE Days called 'Creating Character'. These explore the Christian values of Friendship, Forgiveness and Peace; and Compassion, Service and Community. In an age of uncertainty, we want to help shape a generation of people who are more tolerant and loving of each other.

Since BRF's story began in 1922, we have been making a difference through the Christian faith. Today our creative programmes and resources for schools, individuals and churches impact the lives of thousands of individuals across the UK and overseas. This is thanks, in large part, to the generosity of those who have supported us during their lifetime and through gifts in wills.

If you share our passion for making a difference through the Christian faith, please consider leaving a gift in your will to BRF. Gifts in wills are an important source of income for us and they don't need to be huge to make a real difference. For every £1 we receive, we invest 95p back into charitable activities. Just imagine what we could do over the next century with your help.

For further information about making a gift to BRF in your will, please visit **brf.org.uk/lastingdifference** or contact Sophie on 01865 319700 or email giving@brf.org.uk.

Whatever you can do or give, we thank you for your support.

SHARING OUR VISION – MAKING A GIFT

I would like to make a gift to support BRF. Please use my gift for:

☐ where it is needed most ☐ Barnabas Children's Ministry

☐ Messy Church ☐ Who Let The Dads Out? ☐ The Gift of Years

Title	First name/initials	Surname
Address		
		Postcode
Email		
Telephone		
Signature		Date

giftaid it You can add an extra 25p to every £1 you give.

Please treat as Gift Aid donations all qualifying gifts of money made

☐ today, ☐ in the past four years, ☐ and in the future.

I am a UK taxpayer and understand that if I pay less Income Tax and/or Capital Gains Tax in the current tax year than the amount of Gift Aid claimed on all my donations, it is my responsibility to pay any difference.

☐ My donation does not qualify for Gift Aid.

Please notify BRF if you want to cancel this Gift Aid declaration, change your name or home address, or no longer pay sufficient tax on your income and/or capital gains.

Please complete other side of form ➲

Please return this form to:
BRF, 15 The Chambers, Vineyard, Abingdon OX14 3FE

SHARING OUR VISION – MAKING A GIFT

Regular giving

By Direct Debit:

☐ I would like to make a regular gift of £ [_____] per month/quarter/year.
   Please also complete the Direct Debit instruction on page 159.

By Standing Order:

Please contact Priscilla Kew +44 (0)1235 462305 | giving@brf.org.uk

One-off donation

Please accept my gift of:

☐ £10 ☐ £50 ☐ £100 Other £ [_____]

by (delete as appropriate):

☐ Cheque/Charity Voucher payable to 'BRF'

☐ MasterCard/Visa/Debit card/Charity card

Name on card

Card no. [ ][ ][ ][ ] [ ][ ][ ][ ] [ ][ ][ ][ ] [ ][ ][ ][ ]

Valid from [M][M] [Y][Y] Expires [M][M] [Y][Y]

Security code* [ ][ ][ ] *Last 3 digits on the reverse of the card
ESSENTIAL IN ORDER TO PROCESS YOUR PAYMENT

Signature   Date

We like to acknowledge all donations. However, if you do not wish to receive
an acknowledgement, please tick here ☐

↻ Please complete other side of form

Please return this form to:

BRF, 15 The Chambers, Vineyard, Abingdon OX14 3FE

BRF

The Bible Reading Fellowship is a Registered Charity (233280)

GL0317

GUIDELINES SUBSCRIPTION RATES

Please note our new subscription rates for the coming year. From the May 2017 issue, the new subscription rates will be:

Individual subscriptions
covering 3 issues for under 5 copies, payable in advance
(including postage & packing):

	UK	Europe	Rest of world
Guidelines	£16.50	£24.60	£28.50
Guidelines 3-year subscription (9 issues)	£45.00	N/A	N/A

Group subscriptions
covering 3 issues for 5 copies or more, sent to **one** UK address (post free):

Guidelines	£13.20 per set of 3 issues p.a.

Please note that the annual billing period for group subscriptions runs from 1 May to 30 April.

Overseas group subscription rates
Available on request. Please email enquiries@brf.org.uk.

Copies may also be obtained from Christian bookshops:

Guidelines	£4.40 per copy

All our Bible reading notes can be ordered online by visiting
biblereadingnotes.org.uk/subscriptions

For information about our other Bible reading notes,
and apps for iPhone and iPod touch, visit
biblereadingnotes.org.uk

GUIDELINES INDIVIDUAL SUBSCRIPTION FORM

All our Bible reading notes can be ordered online by visiting
biblereadingnotes.org.uk/subscriptions

☐ I would like to take out a subscription:

Title .... First name/initials .... Surname ....

Address ....

.... Postcode ....

Telephone .... Email ....

Please send *Guidelines* beginning with the January 2018 / May 2018 / September 2018 issue (*delete as appropriate*):

(*please tick box*)

	UK	Europe	Rest of world
Guidelines	☐ £16.50	☐ £24.60	☐ £28.50
Guidelines 3-year subscription	☐ £45.00	N/A	N/A

Total enclosed £ .... (cheques should be made payable to 'BRF')

Please charge my MasterCard / Visa ☐ Debit card ☐ with £ ....

Card no. ☐☐☐☐ ☐☐☐☐ ☐☐☐☐ ☐☐☐☐

Valid from ☐☐ ☐☐   Expires ☐☐ ☐☐   Security code* ☐☐☐

Last 3 digits on the reverse of the card

Signature* .... Date ..../......./.......

*ESSENTIAL IN ORDER TO PROCESS YOUR PAYMENT

To set up a Direct Debit, please also complete the Direct Debit instruction on page 159 and return it to BRF with this form.

Please return this form with the appropriate payment to:
BRF, 15 The Chambers, Vineyard, Abingdon OX14 3FE

To read our terms and find out about cancelling your order, please visit **brfonline.org.uk/terms**.

The Bible Reading Fellowship (BRF) is a Registered Charity (233280)

GL0317

GUIDELINES GIFT SUBSCRIPTION FORM

☐ I would like to give a gift subscription (please provide both names and addresses):

Title .... First name/initials .... Surname ....

Address ....

.... Postcode ....

Telephone .... Email ....

Gift subscription name ....

Gift subscription address ....

.... Postcode ....

Gift message (20 words max. or include your own gift card):

....

....

Please send *Guidelines* beginning with the January 2018 / May 2018 / September 2018 issue (*delete as appropriate*):

(*please tick box*)	UK	Europe	Rest of world
Guidelines	☐ £16.50	☐ £24.60	☐ £28.50
Guidelines 3-year subscription	☐ £45.00	N/A	N/A

Total enclosed £ .... (cheques should be made payable to 'BRF')

Please charge my MasterCard / Visa ☐ Debit card ☐ with £ ....

Card no. ☐☐☐☐ ☐☐☐☐ ☐☐☐☐ ☐☐☐☐

Valid from ☐☐☐☐ Expires ☐☐☐☐ Security code* ☐☐☐

Last 3 digits on the reverse of the card

Signature* .... Date ....../....../......

*ESSENTIAL IN ORDER TO PROCESS YOUR PAYMENT

To set up a Direct Debit, please also complete the Direct Debit instruction on page 159 and return it to BRF with this form.

Please return this form with the appropriate payment to:
BRF, 15 The Chambers, Vineyard, Abingdon OX14 3FE

To read our terms and find out about cancelling your order, please visit **brfonline.org.uk/terms**.

The Bible Reading Fellowship (BRF) is a Registered Charity (233280)

DIRECT DEBIT PAYMENT

You can pay for your annual subscription to our Bible reading notes using Direct Debit. You need only give your bank details once, and the payment is made automatically every year until you cancel it. If you would like to pay by Direct Debit, please use the form opposite, entering your BRF account number under 'Reference number'.

You are fully covered by the Direct Debit Guarantee:

The Direct Debit Guarantee

- This Guarantee is offered by all banks and building societies that accept instructions to pay Direct Debits.

- If there are any changes to the amount, date or frequency of your Direct Debit, The Bible Reading Fellowship will notify you 10 working days in advance of your account being debited or as otherwise agreed. If you request The Bible Reading Fellowship to collect a payment, confirmation of the amount and date will be given to you at the time of the request.

- If an error is made in the payment of your Direct Debit, by The Bible Reading Fellowship or your bank or building society, you are entitled to a full and immediate refund of the amount paid from your bank or building society.

- If you receive a refund you are not entitled to, you must pay it back when The Bible Reading Fellowship asks you to.

- You can cancel a Direct Debit at any time by simply contacting your bank or building society. Written confirmation may be required. Please also notify us.

GL0317

The Bible Reading Fellowship

Instruction to your bank or building society to pay by Direct Debit

Please fill in the whole form using a ballpoint pen and return it to:
BRF, 15 The Chambers, Vineyard, Abingdon OX14 3FE

Service User Number: | 5 | 5 | 8 | 2 | 2 | 9 |

Name and full postal address of your bank or building society

To: The Manager	Bank/Building Society
Address	
	Postcode

Name(s) of account holder(s)

Branch sort code

Bank/Building Society account number

Reference number

Instruction to your Bank/Building Society

Please pay The Bible Reading Fellowship Direct Debits from the account detailed in this instruction, subject to the safeguards assured by the Direct Debit Guarantee. I understand that this instruction may remain with The Bible Reading Fellowship and, if so, details will be passed electronically to my bank/building society.

Signature(s)

Banks and Building Societies may not accept Direct Debit instructions for some types of account.

This page is left blank for your notes.